MEETING

1705

C. G. Jung and E. A. Bennet at Bollingen, 1957.

Meetings with Jung

Conversations recorded
during the years 1946–1961 by

E. A. Bennet

DAIMON
ZÜRICH

Second edition 1985

Cover design and graphics: Joel T. Miskin

ISBN 3-85630-501-7

Copyright © 1985 Daimon Verlag, Postfach,
CH-8024 Zurich, Switzerland

ACKNOWLEDGMENTS

References to the following works in the notes which accompany the text are reprinted here by kind permission of Routledge & Kegan Paul, London, and Princeton University Press, U.S.A. : *The Collected Works of C. G. Jung*, edited by Sir Herbert Read, Michael Fordham and Gerhard Adler; translated by R. F. C. Hull. (Copyright Routledge & Kegan Paul, London, and Princeton University Press, U.S.A., Bollingen Series XX). (The abbreviation *CW* has been used to indicate *Collected Works*). *C. G. Jung: Letters*, edited by Gerhard Adler in collaboration with Aniela Jaffé, translated by R. F. C. Hull; Vol. I: *1906–1950*, and Vol. II: *1951–1961*. (Copyright Routledge & Kegan Paul, London, and Princeton University Press, U.S.A., Bollingen Series XCV).

Permission from William Collins and Routledge & Kegan Paul, London, and from Pantheon Books U.S.A., is acknowledged in quoting from *Memories, Dreams, Reflections,* by C. G. Jung, recorded and edited by Aniela Jaffé, translated by Richard and Clara Winston (Copyright Random House, Inc., 1961).

Quotations from *C. G. Jung: His Myth in Our Time*, by Marie-Louise von Franz, are included by courtesy of the author, and of the C. G. Foundation for Analytical Psychology, New York. (Copyright by the C. G. Jung Foundation for Analytical Psychology, 1975, New York).

Acknowledgment is made also to Miss Barbara Hannah for permission to quote from her biographical memoir, *Jung: His Life and Work*, published by G. P. Putnam's Sons, New York, 1976, and to the copyright owners of quotations which are not listed above.

PREFACE

In the spring of 1946 my husband visited C.G.Jung for the first time since the outbreak of war in 1939 and his account of the conversation began the record of their meetings which was to span the following fourteen years. It is a collection of informal notes, almost always written on the day he describes. While the facts and ideas they contain were expanded in his books, the notes were never altered, nor was anything added to them in retrospect. To widen the context some references are given to Jung's works and letters, and to other relevant writings.

In preparing the text I have been deeply indebted to the friends whose interest and help has set it on its way. My grateful thanks are extended to Dr. Marie-Louise von Franz, who contributed the Introduction and, with Miss Barbara Hannah, read the original manuscript and verified some of the details; to Dorothea Wallis for her helpful comments, and to John Wallis who discussed the editing and also designed the volume.

April 1985   EVELINE BENNET

INTRODUCTION

The notes presented here were written by Dr. Bennet during visits to Professor Jung in the years preceding the publication of his two books, *C. G. Jung*[1] and *What Jung Really Said*.[2] He was a perceptive observer, sensitive to the whole ambience in which he met Jung, and his immediate, spontaneous account of their meetings testifies also to a friendship which lasted nearly thirty years.

Edward Armstrong Bennet was born in Poyntzpass, near Armagh in Northern Ireland, on 21 October 1888. He was educated at Campbell College, Belfast, and studied philosophy and theology at Trinity College, Dublin, where he obtained an honours degree in philosophy. After further studies at Ridley Hall, Cambridge, he was ordained in the Church of England. At the outbreak of the First War he joined the Sixth Northants Regiment as their chaplain, and in 1915 he was awarded the M.C. for conspicuous bravery. The experiences of the war led him to return afterwards to Trinity College where he qualified in medicine in 1925. Later, in 1939, he was awarded the Sc.D. by the same college.

From the start of his medical career Dr. Bennet's interest lay in psychiatry. Soon after 1925 he moved to London and joined the staff of the Tavistock Clinic; he also took up an appointment at the West End Hospital for Nervous Diseases, and within a few years was lecturing regularly on psychological medicine. His work was characterised by a deep concern for people and their suffering – which is probably the basic motivation of all really good doctors.

In his memoirs Jung tells of his experience at the end of his studies in medicine, when he came across a textbook on psychiatry by Krafft-Ebing and read in it that 'psychoses were diseases of the personality'. He writes: 'My excitement was intense … Here alone the two currents of my interest could flow together and in a united stream dig their own bed. Here was the empirical field common to biological and

9

spiritual facts, which I had everywhere sought and nowhere found. Here at last was the place where the collision of nature and spirit became reality.'[3]

The age-old western schism between the philosophical and religious outlooks on one side, and that of the sciences on the other, was united for him in this new dimension: *the reality of the psyche*. From this awareness difficulties developed for Jung because his medical colleagues, including Freud, could seldom understand his interest in religious experiences, and theologians and philosophers failed to comprehend his empirical approach to their ideas, which was inspired by the method of the sciences.

That Dr. Bennet's background included knowledge of theology and philosophy as well as medicine predisposed him to understand and value Jung's approach. He met him first early in the 1930s, and from 1935, at the Tavistock Lectures – when Jung made a great impact on his audience – he maintained contact with him, and over the years did much to establish Jung's ideas in England. Among those attracted to Jung's thought were some who became imitative, and others who sought to 'go beyond Jung'. In contrast, Dr. Bennet's attitude stemmed from inner independence of thought. He remained primarily a true medical psychiatrist, using for each patient the treatment he considered most appropriate; but his most influential work was certainly the personal psychotherapy of individuals on Jungian lines. His perceptive insight, together with his kindness and concern for people, made him an outstanding psychotherapist.

The long association with Jung was interrupted during the years of the Second War when Dr. Bennet served in the Army as command psychiatrist, India Command and 11th Army Group, with the rank of brigadier. In this field he developed a certain disciplined firmness which is an important quality for a psychotherapist. After the war he was invited to join the staff of the Royal Bethlem and Maudsley Hospitals, from which he retired in 1955. He served on the Hypnotism Sub-committee of the British Medical Association in 1953 and on the Medical Sub-committee of the Archbishop of Canterbury's Commission on Spiritual Healing in 1954–55. He was also a member of the Drug Addiction Committee of the B.M.A. from 1955–61. He died on the 7th March 1977; his death was a great loss to his friends, colleagues and patients, and for the Jungian groups he had influenced.

The notes which follow convey no complete picture of Jung's life or thought, but rather they reflect impressions of his everyday life, his conversation, and his natural, spontaneous way of living and thinking. There is frequent mention of his writings – often of books he was currently working on; prominent among them in the closing chapters of the journal is *Memories, Dreams, Reflections,* which was written during the last years of his life. Those who look for extended reading on some of the topics spoken of here will find in these comments alone an indication of the sources available to them.

M.-L. VON FRANZ

REFERENCES

1 E. A. Bennet, *C. G. Jung* (Barrie & Rockliff, London 1961).
2 E. A. Bennet, *What Jung Really Said* (Macdonald, London 1966).
3 C. G. Jung, *Memories, Dreams, Reflections,* Chapter III, 'Student Years', p. 111.

Küsnacht, 29th March 1946

Arriving from Geneva yesterday I was met by car at the station in Zürich and reached the Seestrasse just before one o'clock. With C.G. and Mrs. Jung were their daughter and son-in-law, Marianne and Walther Niehus, and two children, a girl of about sixteen and a boy of six – also C.G.'s secretary, Miss Schmid.

We sat down to a lovely lunch – fish mayonnaise followed by beef, then biscuits, and afterwards coffee on the verandah. Later I had a long talk with C.G. till tea-time, and left about five. He looks very fit, is most alert, and appears in excellent health though he says his heart is a bit weak – he can't do hills and must go slowly upstairs.

He spoke of the sense of isolation in Switzerland in 1940. They were expecting a German invasion, and one day his brother-in-law at Schaffhausen sent a message warning him that the Germans might come that night. He took his wife and daughter and his daughter-in-law (who was eight months pregnant) to a *refugium* in east Switzerland by car. The general plan was that in the event of invasion the Swiss would evacuate the flat ground near Zürich, and fight in the hills where they would blow up the railway tunnels, the Gottard and others. This was a big factor, a trump card – Switzerland would be useless to the Germans without communications to Italy.

He listened daily to the B.B.C. and knew that England was the only hope, and that they would never give in.

He said that until 1935 it had seemed possible, in Germany and Italy, that some good could come from Nazi-ism. Germany was transformed; instead of roads crowded with people without work, all was changed and peaceful. Then he saw other things and knew it was evil. He began to speak against it – as at the Oxford Congress[1] for instance – and did so increasingly. He showed me an American article which had been falsely translated, misquoting him on the subject: his phrase 'looking with amazed eyes' (at the trend of events in Europe) had been transcribed as 'looking with admiring eyes'. He said it had been answered. He became so outspoken in his criticisms of Germany that Mrs. Jung was afraid he would get into trouble, with so much German influence in Zürich. Referring to the rumours of his so-called Nazi sympathies, C.G. told me that his name was on the black list in Germany because of his views, and that he would certainly have been shot at once had he fallen into Nazi hands.[2]

He said that at the Oxford Congress he had asked Göring[3] if he thought there would be a war, and Göring replied, 'Well, if there is there will be a round table conference later.' C.G. added that this would never have happened had Germany won.

Of Russia – he said Stalin was clever and no fool. He had feared much when the Russians came into the war; but then he had a striking dream, of which he told me a part:

He was in a vast field with, in the distance, buildings like barracks. The place was filled with hordes of buffalos (i.e. Germans). He was on a mound, and Hitler was on another mound. He felt that as long as he fixed his gaze on Hitler all would be well. Then he saw a cloud of dust in the distance, and horsemen – Cossacks – rounding up the buffalos and driving them out of the field. Then he woke and was glad, for he knew that Germany would be beaten by Russia. This, he said, was a collective dream, and very important.

Various chat. I told him of the Stalingrad sword incident[4] and of Chamberlain forgetting his umbrella at Godesburgh.[5] C.G. was most interested in the former, and said of the latter that when people leave without an object that belongs to them it means that they are unconscious of something – as patients forget their notebook or bag etc.; it is not simply an indication that they don't want to go, or want to come back.

He has had a long correspondence with Father Victor White[6] of Blackfriars, Oxford, and is very impressed by him and his learning. They publish a magazine, *Blackfriars*.

Both he and Mrs. Jung told me that he was publishing all his papers about Germany and the Nazis; the book is already in print and will be translated.[7]

REFERENCES

1 The Tenth International Medical Congress for Psychotherapy, held at Oxford, July 29th to August 2nd, 1938.

2 E. A. Bennet, *C. G. Jung*, p. 60, and the reference there to the article by Ernest Harms, 'Carl Gustav Jung – Defender of Freud and the Jews', *Psychiatric Quarterly* (1946), Vol. 20, p. 199.

   Barbara Hannah also writes fully of Jung's attitude to the Nazis in *Jung: His Life and Work*, Chapter 11, 'Storm Clouds Over Europe 1933–1937'.

3 Professor M. H. Göring of Wuppertal, cousin of Reichminister Hermann Göring.

4 The incident occurred in 1943 at the presentation of the Stalingrad sword. The blade of the sword was engraved, in English and Russian, '*To the steel-hearted citizens of Stalingrad, the gift of King George VI, in token of the homage of the British people*'– a gift which honoured the Russian victory at Stalingrad. The sword was made by craftsmen of the Goldsmiths' Company and was described in a contemporary article in *The Studio* as 'perhaps the most important work of art of our generation, owing to its intrinsic beauty, fine craftsmanship, and to the circumstances in which it was produced.' The design was that of a Crusader's sword, the gold-bound grip shielded by a finely ornamented crossguard and surmounted by a pommel of carved rock crystal set in a gold rose. When Churchill, Roosevelt and Stalin met at Teheran on 29 November 1943, Churchill presented the sword to Stalin, on behalf of the King and the British people, at a simple and impressive ceremony. The sequel was cut from the official film of the proceedings, but according to eye-witnesses, when Stalin, after receiving the sword, turned to hand it to Marshal Voroshilov beside him, it slid from the scabbard, and only a quick movement by Voroshilov saved the priceless rock crystal pommel from destruction. (These details are given by courtesy of the Worshipful Company of Goldsmiths. The story of the Stalingrad sword is fully described in *The Worshipful Company of Goldsmiths as Patrons of their Craft 1919–1953*, by George Hughes, published by the Company, 1965).

5 That Chamberlain forgot his umbrella after his meeting with Hitler at Godesburgh was noticed, not only because it had come to be associated with him as an inseparable part of his attire, but also because he had himself drawn attention to it, using it as a symbol of unity and protection. Thus, in replying to the vote of thanks after a speech at Blackburn in February 1939, he remarked, '... it is the greatest possible encouragement and support to me to think that I have under that old umbrella so many of my fellow countrymen and countrywomen who believe with me that peace is the greatest blessing that any country can enjoy ... that by determination and persistence we can secure that peace for ourselves and the world.' (Reported in *The Times*, 23 February 1939, under the heading, 'That Old Umbrella').

6 Father Victor White O.P., S.T.B., author of *God and the Unconscious*, Foreword by C. G. Jung. The letters mentioned here are published in *C. G. Jung: Letters*, Vol. I.

7 C. G. Jung, *Essays on Contemporary Events*, first published in London in 1947. See also *Civilization in Transition*, CW Vol. 10, III.

August, the time of the International Conference[1] in Zürich when I stayed with the Jungs at Küsnacht.

10th August 1946

During our conversation at breakfast C.G. spoke of the Virgin Birth, and said that when he met William Temple[2] he had told him that he hadn't been clear about the Virgin Birth, but a bit deviating (here he gave an inimitable movement of the hands and shoulders as if shaping and moulding something to suit circumstances, like the movement a person makes in contriving to get something to fit). Temple had agreed: he hadn't 'got it', and the Anglican Church hadn't either – it was apologetic and tended to pass it over. C.G. went on to say that it must be understood psychologically; it made no sense to think of it as if Mrs. Jones had a baby but no husband or man. No, *the Virgin was the archetypal figure of the soul of man, the anima*, and it is only in the soul of man that God can be born, where else could it be? This is comprehended, he said, by the Catholic Church, but not by others. It is a big psychological truth, symbolised by the figure of the Virgin Mary.[3]

At dinner Hugh Crichton-Miller was there, and also an Italian doctor who left early. Afterwards we had a long talk with C.G. and Mrs. Jung in the sitting room next to the dining room, where there is a big blue-green stove with tiles painted with designs from an ancient book on natural science which C.G. showed us.

The Italian doctor had spoken of a curious situation which arose during the war. A soldier was wounded and had to be fed through a fistula into his stomach. Could he receive the wafer at Mass through the fistula, or must it be taken by mouth? It was decided that the essential thing was the assimilation, and therefore it could be taken through the fistula.

The topic of the Virgin Birth was raised again, and C.G. emphasised the importance of dogma – facts which were true.[4] The Roman Catholic Church does not bother about people 'believing', as the Protestants do; the people are 'in the Church'. The Mass is said in Latin;[5] it remains unchanged through the ages, and so it is with dogmas. At the Mass people present may be talking to one another and not following it; but when the bell rings, the *sanctus* bell, they cross themselves. There is grace to all in the vicinity; it accumulated, as it were, in the place over centuries, and people 'got it'. The Protestant Church lost this at the Reformation; they became rational – must *understand*, not feel, and this was bad. They rely only on the Bible and faith, and this was not enough. But there was a numinosity about the Roman Catholic Mass, and about anything which gives expression to psychic reality, and people 'got it'.[6]

He told us of his Terry Lectures at Yale.[7] He dislikes crowds and dislikes majorities, so at Yale he asked for a small hall in which to lecture. But the Dean said he had arranged to use the big hall for the first lecture, as a lot of people would come to it out of curiosity who would not come again, and for the second lecture they could move to a smaller hall. At C.G.'s first lecture the big hall was not full; it held three thousand, and about six or seven hundred people were there. Then, to his surprise, when he asked for the small hall for his second lecture the Dean said they must have the big hall, and when he went in he found it full. At the third lecture it was crowded with people standing and sitting everywhere. 'Yet,' he said, 'it was very difficult stuff and probably none of them understood it; but they "got it" – the numinous quality.' When he went out after the last lecture he found the Dean's wife getting tea with tears streaming down her face. C.G. thought it must be some domestic trouble. She apologised and said she was crying. 'Yes, I see,' said C.G., and asked if he should withdraw. 'Oh no,' she answered, 'I didn't understand a word of it, but I feel it.' 'That's it,' remarked C.G., 'she got what was there – like the Mass – didn't understand, but was *in it*.'

REFERENCES

1 The International Conference for Analytical Psychology, held in Zürich in August 1946.

2 Dr. William Temple (1881–1946), Archbishop of York (1929) and of Canterbury (1942).

17

3 C.G. Jung, *Psychology and Religion*, CW Vol. 11, VI, *Answer to Job*; in para. 553
   he writes of '... the strange supposition that a thing is true only if it presents itself as a *physical* fact. Thus some people believe it to be physically true that Christ
   was born as the son of a virgin, while others deny this. ... Yet they could easily
   reach agreement if only they dropped the word "physical".'

   C. G. Jung: Letters, Vol. I. On 23 June 1947 Jung wrote to Pastor Werner
   Niederer: 'It must be understood that there is *objective psychic existence*, and that
   psychological explanation is not necessarily psychologizing, i.e. subjectivizing.
   The concept of dogma must be reviewed. I once reproached the late Dr. Temple,
   Archbishop of Canterbury, with the fact that in the "Doctrine of the Church of
   England" the dogma of the Virgin Birth is hedged about with qualifications and
   thus thrown in doubt. ... Dogma is *credibile quia ineptum* [credible because ab-
   surd: Tertullian]. To be understood at all it must be understood *typice* – in
   modern terms, *archetypally*. In our example Virgin=ANIMA *quae non novit
   virum* [the soul which did not know man]. She does not conceive by man, but
   conceives God himself by God himself. That seems to me much better and more
   understandable, for such things can be observed and experienced.'

   C. G. Jung, *Memories, Dreams, Reflections*, Chapter XII, 'Late Thoughts',
   pp. 309–11.
4 C. G. Jung, *Psychology and Religion*, CW Vol. 11, I, paras. 81, 82: '... dogma
   owes its continued existence and its form on the one hand to so-called "revealed"
   or immediate experiences of the "Gnosis" [knowledge of God] – for instance,
   the God-man, the Cross, the Virgin Birth ... and on the other hand to the cease-
   less collaboration of many minds over many centuries. ... Yet the Christian
   images I have mentioned are not peculiar to Christianity alone. ... They occur
   just as often in pagan religions ... and can reappear spontaneously in all sorts of
   variations as psychic phenomena, just as in the remote past they originated in
   visions, dreams, or trances. Ideas like these are never invented. ... Dogma is like
   a dream, reflecting the spontaneous and autonomous activity of the unconscious.
   ... Dogma lasts for untold centuries ... and expresses the soul more completely
   than a scientific theory.'
5 The English version of the Roman Catholic Mass was introduced in 1964.
6 C. G. Jung, *Psychology and Religion*, CW Vol. 11, III, *Transformation Symbolism in the Mass*.
7 Jung's Terry Lectures of 1937 are published in *Psychology and Religion*, CW Vol.
   11, Part I.

Küsnacht, 3rd June 1946

Talk with C.G.[1] We must descend if we are to ascend (St. Augustine).

About parables: the parable of the unjust steward – he must save his face, that's the bug. Parables are marvellous when read psychologically; burying the talent – not using what we have because of laziness or shyness, or lack of knowledge.

Then on to the doctrine of the trinity as mirrored in atomic physics; the atom is invisible, like the invisible things of the psyche, of the unconscious.[2] He is working on the relationship of atomic physics and the unconscious.

Of the Virgin Birth: God is born in the soul of man. Christ was illegitimate and born virtually on a dunghill, yet the Son of God. When you show people the myth it is therapeutic – they see the link with a wider experience, that they are not alone.[3]

His illness was the result of working too hard and having two things, his patients and his writing. Many tasks worried him because they were unfinished; then working at them he would be interrupted by the claims of patients. The disorder lasted only about a week; but yesterday he was not well and could not see me.

He told me of a student who asked his professor, 'How do you know there is a God?' The professor had no answer and came and asked Jung! This man is a great preacher, yet it's all words, no real knowledge. C.G. said, 'I would have loved that question – there you have a student who can learn something.'

REFERENCES

1 The original notes of this conversation are sparse and the text given here contains a few verbal amendments.

2 C. G. Jung, *Psychology and Religion*, CW Vol. 11, II, *A Psychological Approach to the Dogma of the Trinity*, para. 279: 'To use an analogy from physics, the Holy Ghost could be likened to the stream of photons arising out of the destruction of

matter, while the "Father" would be the primordial energy that promotes the formation of protons and electrons with their positive and negative charges. This, as the reader will understand, is not an explanation, but an analogy which is possible because the physicist's models ultimately rest on the same archetypal foundations that also underlie the speculations of the theologian. Both are psychology, and it too has no other foundation.'

3 In the opening paragraphs of his 'Prologue' to *Memories, Dreams, Reflections*, Jung writes: 'What we are to our inward vision, and what man appears to be *sub specie aeternitatis*, can only be expressed by way of myth. Myth is more individual and expresses life more precisely than does science.'

Jung's use of the word *myth* as a central idea giving meaning to life is clear in the conversation of 15 July 1957.

The thought behind his brief remarks in this conversation is found towards the end of *Memories, Dreams, Reflections*, Chapter XII, 'Late Thoughts', pp. 310–12, and in the closing paragraphs of *Answer to Job, Psychology and Religion*, CW Vol. 11, VI, paras. 755ff.

SUMMER 1949

Bollingen, 25th July 1949
It was here, on this day, that I first met Victor White. He was bathing in the lake when I arrived and I also had a bathe, so we met in the water.

After tea we sat at a table in the front garden with C.G. and Mrs. Jung, a grand-daughter of theirs, and Father Victor White. C.G. and I had a talk for over two hours sitting by the edge of the lake. White had seen a snake in the water and as we talked we saw the snake twice; it swam along rather beautifully, about a yard long.

I spoke to C.G. of a dream a patient had told me: he had a basin filled with golden-coloured water and in it were some golden fish; he had to drink some of the water. A fish fell out and he replaced it. C.G. said it meant that some of the unconscious was within reach and that he could take from it. The fish was the symbol of the unconscious life, like the Christ.

27th July 1949
I arrived at Bollingen at three o'clock and had a bathe. The Jungs were there with Father White and their grandchild Sybil. Lovely bathe. Sybil had a kettle being boiled on twigs.

Then a chat with C.G. He spoke of the stages of life, for I had mentioned the importance to the younger generation of having grandparents. He had not known his; he said his grandmother died in 1864.

He went on to speak of obsessional people as always fearing death; they want to remain adolescent and never grow up. Some patients (he cited a case) may even decline to shake hands with the doctor, who has to do with death. Adolescents have everything ahead of them; their decisions will be taken in the future. And the obsessional person is reluctant to decide anything. Nothing must be fixed for that would mean life was getting on, so there is hesitation over any decision, *it must be possible to alter it, undo it – it is always reversible*. Through their symptoms they retain an immature attitude and neglect their work, their duties in life.

He mentioned the case of a woman who felt compelled to play incessantly on the piano, and to play a different tune with each hand; this she did until she fainted and then she would start again. She came to him pleading for help. He told her that she did not want to get well, and he would show her this and see how she would then react. He asked her to carry out an experiment: for one day to do all the things a wife should do – get her husband's breakfast, attend to his clothes and her household duties – just for one day. She returned still asking for help. 'What about our experiment?' he asked, 'Did you do it?' 'Yes,' she said. 'And did you have any symptoms?' 'No, none at all.' 'Well there it is!' he said. Her reply was, 'But it was so boring!'

He also referred to the case of a man with an obsessional neurosis who had lived self-indulgently for years, drawing on the financial support of a schoolteacher who loved him though he knew his expenses were beyond her means (cited in *Modern Man*, I think).[1] He had had a long Freudian analysis. This man blamed C.G. for moralising when he told him, 'There is your moral fault', for we all have a moral side.

He went on to speak of Freud and mentioned the importance to him of his dogmas.[2] After many years without neurosis people can find themselves confronted with problems. In psychoanalysis they go back to early childhood things and in so doing escape from the real immediate situation. It's like a river: in the early stages there are the little tributaries, and as it flows on the channel deepens and the side streams dry up. But if the river is blocked in its course the water rises and flows back into the old disused channels again. But *they are not the cause of the situation*; the cause is the block in the river. And of course patients love to go back and back for this leads away from their problem, and there are always the endless things of childhood to talk of. But in this both analyst and patient are blinded to the present problem.

I asked, 'What cures?' and he said, 'You can cure with anything if you believe in it; you can cure neuroses with hypnotism, or with a walking stick, if that is what you believe in. Freud was kind to people and gave them his interest, that was what cured and that is what always cures – the human contact. What you believe in is what cures.'[3]

He talked of *absolute knowledge* –'What a term, *absolute*!' He meant by it the real truth that we touch on now and then. We are related to everything –'to that tree'– for we are all part of nature, and it makes a pattern. We cling to our consciousness as something big; but beyond it we can get into the stream of nature, the real unconscious.

Perhaps we cannot understand a patient – we are completely stuck; then we may get a hint from an unexpected source, for instance from astrology: 'I don't care whether it's "true" or not, I'm interested only in the fact that it can, and does, give us a hint.' He mentioned also the *I Ching*, and an intuitive mediaeval system he had come across recently.[4] He added that one could test these things only with discrimination; 'But one can see at times if they work,' he said, 'and when they do it's a help; we must get beyond our heads.'

12th August 1949
To Bollingen again. After tea we sat in the tower room. Later I had a talk with C.G. in the study upstairs. He spoke of *unmindful coincidences*, that is coincidences *which could not have been anticipated*. He gave an example of a dream he had recently of Churchill, and next day he read that Churchill had just passed through Switzerland. He added that on two previous occasions he had dreamt of Churchill and each time he had read the following day that Churchill had been in Switzerland at the time, or passing through; once was in 1944, when Churchill had alighted to refuel at Geneva on his way to Greece.[5]

In this context of *synchronicity* he mentioned the old notion of Correspondence (Swedenborg).[6] He said the fundamental concept in physics was space, time and causation; when you had these three you had all that was needed. But there is more, namely that things happen together at a certain time. He alluded by way of illustration to the decay of radium, that after about 1400 years the granule of radium had gone. It diminishes at a certain rate; space, time and causation do not account for this. The comparison he gave was as if, say, sixty men sit down to dinner and each has a card with a time on it at which he must rise and go. One gets up, perhaps at two minutes past four, and another at four minutes past, and so on, irregularly, and seemingly at random. Gradually the room becomes empty. So it is with radium, it just 'fades away'. Or the ice crystals which form on the window; no one sees two alike. Each atom knows its place; previously all were water, then there is the ice crystal with its axial pattern, quite perfect, and unpremeditated (by us). It seems, like radium, to follow laws of which we know nothing, as though there was some 'absolute knowledge' in nature.

REFERENCES

1 C. G. Jung, *Modern Man in Search of a Soul*, Chapter IX.

2 E. A. Bennet, *C. G. Jung*, pp. 47–48: 'Again and again Freud insisted that a dogma was an essential safeguard to prevent the black cloud or black flood of occultism from swamping his original work, which, quite rightly, he valued highly. By this Freud sometimes meant religious ideas, but more usually the phrase referred to the unconscious which, in itself, apart from the personal circumstances of the individual, had no meaning for Freud, and so he was disposed to depreciate, to defeat, or overcome it and take it, so to speak, on his own terms.'

3 *C. G. Jung: Letters*, Vol. II. In his letter to Dr. D. Cappon of 15 March 1954, Jung writes: 'One has cured neurosis by the most astonishing means long before our modern psychology. If there are no technical means, it is the sincerity of the doctor's attitude and his willingness to help that restore the impaired wholeness of the patient. ... The successful therapeutic attitude always expects of you that you really do your best, no matter how good or how bad it is, or what kind of technique you apply. Only you must be sure that you do the best you know.'

4 The system referred to is *geomancy*, an ancient divinatory technique based on quaternally structured 'information'. It originated in Islam and in course of time spread throughout Europe. The process of divination is described by Marie-Louise von Franz in *Number and Time* (Northwestern University Press 1974), Chapter 7, pp. 117–19.

5 Churchill flew to Athens on Christmas Day 1944 to discuss the Greek crisis with Field Marshal Earl Alexander of Tunis and Archbishop Damaskinos.

6 Emanuel Swedenborg, *The True Christian Religion (Vera Christina Religio)*, 1771.
   C. G. Jung: Letters, Vol. II. In a letter to Dr. John Raymond Smythies of 29 February 1952, Jung writes: 'In my essay on synchronicity ... I propose a new (really a very old) principle of explanation, *viz.* synchronicity, which is a new term for the time-hallowed ... *correspondentia*. I go back in a way to Leibniz, the last mediaeval thinker with holistic judgment: he explained the phenomenon by four principles: space, time, causality, and correspondence. We have dropped the latter long ago (though Schopenhauer took it up again, disguised as causality). I hold that there is *no causal explanation for psi-phenomena*. Terms like thought-transmission, telepathy, clairvoyance, mean nothing. How can one imagine a causal explanation for a case of precognition?'

Bollingen, 12th September 1950
Sitting by the lake. C.G. spoke of the need for knowledge; we have to
know a lot, for example about symbols, and the contents of the unconscious. When people are confronted with strange or overwhelming inner experiences they may wonder if they are mad, or think they
are 'different', separate. But when the significance of the experience
is shown to them, and its content understood – for instance parts of a
dream, or a picture – their anxiety is relieved and they feel less isolated. We must know these things and impart the knowledge.[1]

We spoke of the *shadow* and I said it puzzled some people. He said
it was very simple: in analysis it is the first thing constellated by the
unconscious; behind it, further from consciousness, is the anima (or
animus) and other collective material. The shadow can represent the
whole of the unconscious – that is both personal and archetypal contents – or just the personal material which was in the background and
not recognised, not wanted. But it has to come forward and be assimilated into consciousness, it is essential.[2]

He said he had learned never to start an interview beyond a few
pleasantries –'How are you?'– but to wait for the patient, because the
instincts, the archetypes, lie in between and we don't know what may
be there. But at times in conversation some topic occurs to him for no
apparent reason, and he talks about it and finds it is just the right
thing. For instance the other day he began talking to a woman doctor
about his African tour and snakes, and wondered why he was telling
her all this; then it turned out to be absolutely relevant for he discovered that she was deeply interested in these things. So we wait and
the instincts guide us.

Commenting on a patient's dream he said that when people become
too introverted it can happen that they think too much of the past.
'People do this and don't expect much of the future; they need to de-

velop expectancy – something fresh can happen.'

C.G. looks very well. After talking to him I had a chat with Toni Wolff on the terrace. Before I left she got me some lunch. We lit a fire in the grate and heated some coffee and I carried it to the terrace with some bread and cheese. The place has a very restful re-creative atmosphere.

As I left I passed C.G. and said goodbye. He was lying on a *chaise-longue* reading in the place where we had been talking. I write this now in glorious sunshine sitting on the bank by the side of the road just above the Tower still, as it were, in the restful unhurried atmosphere of it all.

14th September 1950

We spoke of Korea, and also of Communism. This, C.G. thought, had arisen because of the failure of the Church. The Church has had its *gestapo* – the Inquisition – and its domination; wordly power it always used badly, kept people down and poor. But the spiritual power of the Church has fallen, and Communism is the opposite: it has arisen as the glorification of the *materia*. Hence the new Roman dogma,[3] the deification of matter, *materia*. This is the point, and it is the quaternity, and the feminine principle.[4]

We talked again of the shadow. He said, 'Yes, it represents everything that is obscure, and it can be personal or collective, we just have to observe it and see.' He spoke of it as all that was not realised; it could be good or bad. He spoke also of a multiplicity of women in dreams, a plurality of animas, because man's attitude could be collective in this.

I asked about the origin of his work on types and he said this began entirely by studying Freud and Adler; the one was rather extraverted (Freud) and the other rather introverted (Adler). At this time he (Jung) abandoned all desire for a career; it was possible for him to do this economically, and he decided to find out what we were really dealing with in the mind. He came to see Freud and Adler as having entirely different approaches.[5]

15th September 1950

I asked C.G. about the Christmas tree; he said it was a great symbol because it was the life growing in winter, the winter solstice, and that is what Christ is, the light in the darkness. But the tree can be many things – phallic, or the unconscious.

I asked what a blind person's conception of archetypal ideas would be. He said he had no experience of this; certainly blind people would need to express the archetypes but it was difficult to know in what form – for example the horse or the ford; it was hard to say how these would be experienced without vision.

We spoke of Kant. He said he had quoted Kant, who had a notion of the unconscious and of the obscurity of what things were – *Ding an sich* – we just don't know what things really are in themselves, we have only our impressions of them.

We talked sitting under a canvas roof he had rigged up on the terrace.

16th September 1950

Cold, so we sat in the upper room. He spoke of his house.[6] He had on the table the little oil lamp he used when he wrote about the association tests,[7] and always used here – a very soft light. He would not have electric light installed, or the telephone. He had built the house like those of mediaeval times with thick stone walls and small windows, so when you are inside you are contained; if you want to see more you can go out. He spoke with much feeling of all these old things and I wondered about more recent times. He said we need a certain distance between us and events. He found it difficult to keep fully in touch with the implications of what was happening now, for instance the atom bomb; hence the need to get apart, get quiet, in this place.

He values the things he has to do here, the necessary things, little jobs; they are not a waste of time. We get emptied by too much work and these trivial things restore us.

People are too busy to live, but what do they do with their time, the time they save? It is better to live and *be* someone and not get absorbed in activity all the time.

I referred to Heraclitus, and he said Heraclitus knew a lot and he had got the notion of *enantiodromia*[8] from him. It was important to have a philosophic background and to know the theories of cognition.

He spoke also of Descartes, and of Descartes' dream which com-

27

pensated for his one-sided attitude. This is mentioned in a book he has written on synchronicity.[9] A physicist in Zürich is writing on this with him, from the physicist's point of view. They are having difficulty in getting photo-copies of some manuscript which is in the British Museum. He said this work with the physicist on synchronicity was the last of such writing he would do; it required tremendous concentration and took too much out of him. He had decided to do no work for a year, except what he wanted.

He told me his wife had started to learn Latin, and also some natural science, after her fifth child went to school. Now she can read all the mediaeval Latin texts.

He used to wonder how he would ever read all the books he had: 'I didn't know I would have so long, and now I can read.' He mentioned a doctor who never read anything but medical journals; then he retired, and there was nothing to live for – life was empty, had come to an end, and he died.

Of archetypes: they are the way instinct shows itself. It was ridiculous for Freud to say there was only one kind of energy, *we don't know what energy is*. So he himself hesitated to use the word and used 'libido' instead. We see only the manifestations of energy. It was rubbish to think sex could be the only drive; those who said that were just ignorant, knew nothing.

He referred to the comfort a patient got from the idea that his illness was because of something in the past, in the parents perhaps. But he has the illness *now*. If a man has a bullet in his leg he may find out who shot the bullet, but *he* has it in his leg and it is this which must be dealt with. We cannot help simply by showing him that someone shot at him; we are driven to think of the present problem and to deal with it. The patient has the neurosis *now*, the parents haven't got it.

Speaking of astrology, C.G. said he did not concern himself in the least with whether it was true or false. All that he found of value was that it could give a hint, some indication of things he did not know. And so it was with graphology.

He spoke of his concepts as purely hypothetical, only hypotheses, and if better ones came along he would accept them. As to what things *really* were we just didn't know, we could only try to find out as far as was possible.

He was wearing drill trousers (old) and jack boots, or rather high laced boots, very thick and tough looking, and a wind jacket, plus his green apron. Just going out to work in his garden I think, but he sat and smoked and talked.

REFERENCES

1 In *Memories, Dreams, Reflections*, Chapter VI, 'Confrontation with the Unconscious', Jung wrote of a number of his own impressive dreams which illustrate the kind of experience spoken of here; for instance the disturbing dreams and visions which troubled him in the months immediately preceding the outbreak of the First War, and his dream of Siegfried and the primitive man. Both examples are mentioned in these conversations, on 8 July 1957 and 30 August 1956 respectively.

2 C. G. Jung, *Aion*, CW Vol. 9, Part II, Chapter II, 'The Shadow', and Chapter III, 'The Syzygy: Anima and Animus'.

   His concept of the *archetype* is summarised in *Civilization in Transition*, CW Vol. 10, VI, *A Psychological View of Conscience*, para. 847.

3 The bodily Assumption of the Virgin Mary into heaven was declared a dogma of the Catholic faith by Pope Pius XII in 1950.

   C. G. Jung: Letters, Vol. II: in a letter of 17 March 1951 Jung writes at length of the significance of this declaration, which he considered 'the most important symbological event since the Reformation ...'.

4 C. G. Jung, *Psychology and Religion*, CW Vol. 11, II, *A Psychological Approach to the Dogma of the Trinity*, Chapter 5, 'The Problem of the Fourth'.

   Marie-Louise von Franz, *C. G. Jung: His Myth in Our Time*, pp. 230–31: 'In the gnostic interpretation of the Christ-symbol, as well as those of the alchemical stone and the Mercurius and Anthropos images, the Self emerges as a *natural* symbol of wholeness. It is in contrast to the dogmatic Christ-image, in that the latter contains nothing – or scarcely anything – of the dark, the feminine, the material. It is therefore understandable that the mediaeval theologians should have occupied themselves with the *body* of Christ, and that the mediaeval Grail legends revolve around the idea of Christ's blood in the Grail vessel, because the image of the resurrection body did not satisfy them. That is why the whole discussion was taken up again at the time of the announcement of the dogma of the Assumption of Mary. Through Mary's assumption and coronation, the masculine triad in heaven is completed by a fourth, feminine being. Thus a quaternity is constituted, representing a genuine totality symbol, not merely a postulated one.'

5 C. G. Jung, *Psychological Types*, CW Vol. 6.

   C. G. Jung, *Memories, Dreams, Reflections*, Chapter VII, 'The Work', p. 198.

   E. A. Bennet, *C. G. Jung*, Chapter 5, 'Introverts and Extraverts', in which he mentions Jung's *Two Essays on Analytical Psychology*, with the comment: 'It is worth noting that these essays, in their original form, give the earliest statement on the theory of the collective psyche, the notion of "pairs of opposites" and of psychological types.'

6 Jung's house at Bollingen.

7 *C. G. Jung, Experimental Researches*, CW Vol. 2, Part I, *Studies in Word Associa-tion*. These papers were written during the years 1904–1909.

8 E. A. Bennet, *What Jung Really Said*, Chapter 4, 'Dreams'. Writing of Jung's principle of compensation in dream interpretation (p. 92): 'Jung ... was con-siderably influenced by parts of the teaching of Heraclitus, the Greek philos-opher of about 500 B.C. ... and his doctrine of eternal flux, uninterrupted motion and change. All comes and goes, from life death, from death life. When a one-sided attitude persists, inevitably the opposite attitude comes to the fore in an automatic attempt to restore a balanced attitude. This to and fro process, which governs what may seem to be chance occurrence, Heraclitus called ... *enantio-dromia*, a tendency towards the opposite (*enantios*, opposite, and *dromos*, a quick movement). Nothing remains fixed, unaltered.'

9 C. G. Jung, *The Structure and Dynamics of the Psyche*, CW Vol. 8, VII, *Syn-chronicity: An Acausal Connecting Principle*, para. 937: 'Herein lay the great mistake of the Cartesians, "that they took no account of perceptions which are not apperceived."'

   Marie-Louise von Franz, 'The Dream of Descartes', published in *Timeless Documents of the Soul*, by Jacohsohn, von Franz and Hurwitz (Northwestern University Press 1968). Jung had intended, originally, to include this in his book on synchronicity.

SUMMER 1951

Bollingen, 20th June 1951

We sat in the alcove on the terrace under the canvas cover. As before, C.G. was in country attire, his boots laced with string to just below the knee, drill trousers shoved into them; apron hung round his neck and tucked to one side, and a leather coat with a jumper inside, and an old hat. He makes an impressive figure.

He told me of the stone he had just carved. It stands on a pedestal at the side of the house, near the new wall which was being built when I was here last year. The stone was brought from the quarry on the opposite side of the lake. A single piece was needed to finish the wall at one corner and the size was carefully measured. When C.G. saw the stone coming in the boat he realised it was not the right size for the wall. But then his heart leapt – it was a perfect cube! 'That's the very thing I want!' He felt it was miraculous.[1] He had the stone put in place and has carved three faces of it. On the front is an inscription in Greek characters and a small figure, a *homunculus*. The right face, in Latin, commemorates his seventy-fifth birthday expressing gratitude for all life had given; it is as follows:

Hic lapis exilis extat pretio
Quoque vilis. Spernitur a stultis
Amatur plus ab edoctis.
In Memoriam Natus Di
EIL XXV C. G. Jung
Ex gratitudine fecit et posuit
            MCML

The third face is carved in condensed mediaeval Latin – impossible to read unless one knew the abbreviations. He learned these, he said, in order to read certain mediaeval texts.

Then he talked of *types*, and especially of the functions. I asked about the correlation of functions or types and neuroses of different kinds. He said this would be very difficult, for we get introverted hysterics, and we just can't say why a neurosis is as it is. Probably there is much in mutation, or in the family pattern of the father or mother; but it seems less probable that it fits in with a special type or function, although this may come into it a bit.

I told him I had been asked to write a brief note about him for the *British Medical Journal*[2] and he said, 'Whatever you say make it clear that I have no dogma, I'm still open and haven't got things fixed.'

He went on to talk of Freud's insistence on dogma; to him it was absolutely necessary. C.G. said that Freud did a great work in exposing the working of the mind in repression; but his need to hold to his dogma led him to make everything fit his theories, for instance dreams: if they did not fit in one way then they had to fit in another. He always treated Freud with respect and called him Professor. He said Freud had no notion of the anima. I spoke of archaic ideas and archetypes, and he said certainly Freud had some of these ideas in a partial way, but he made no use of them.[3] In 1905 he had written to Freud saying that while repression was valuable it did not explain all the facts; there was also the *autonomous psyche*, the complex, and this acted on its own apart from repression. Freud did not like the idea of the autonomous psyche, but the complex was a demonstrable fact and it did act on its own.[4]

22nd June 1951

We spoke of groups, and C.G. said he thought it important in a group of doctors that there should be some lay people also, it keeps a balance.

He went on to talk of interviews. He regards an interview with a patient as a social occasion; if the person has a neurosis that is something more, but people should be regarded as normal and met socially. Speaking of intuitive people, he said it was important for them to get down to some task and make it real, 'Otherwise they are like someone looking at that mountain over there through a telescope, and the next thing is they feel they have been there. But they haven't, they must do the work.'

I asked about connections between organic disease and neuroses, and he said the links were not clear. He mentioned that in free association tests breathing was restricted when a complex was touched and that this could be related to TB. He had often treated people with TB psychologically, and when their breathing improved, became deeper, they got better. The restriction in breathing affected the apex of the lungs. Freudians treat the sickness – put the patients on a couch with a rug over them, then they are in the sickness. He doesn't believe in using a couch, but looks on patients as healthy people interfered with by their neurosis. Also if you have a dogma then *you always know*, everything can be explained. But if you haven't then you must find out, and every person is different. So psychopathology is difficult and you can't fit people into your preconceived ideas.

REFERENCES

1 This was because of the significance of the cube as a symbol of wholeness and completion at the time of Jung's seventy-fifth birthday. The impressive quality of the stone is evident in the photograph of it reproduced in *C. G. Jung: Letters*, Vol. II, Plate VIII, facing p. 399.

2 E. A. Bennet, 'A Great Thinker', *British Medical Journal* (1952), I, p. 314.

3 E. A. Bennet, *C. G. Jung*, Chapter 6, p. 92: 'We should remember Freud's statement (in *An Autobiographical Study*, p. 124) that his ideas on the activities of the primal horde [published as *Totem and Taboo*] came to his mind as a "hypothesis, or I would rather say, vision". It is true that Freud's acceptance of non-personal features in the psyche had no observable effect on his system of thought. ... He noted the impersonal facts and passed on. ... In looking back to the parting of Freud and Jung we can reflect sadly that if Freud had followed up his observations on the archaic heritage of the individual he might have found himself in agreement with Jung's conclusion about the collective unconscious. ...'

4 C. G. Jung, *Experimental Researches*, CW Vol. 2. In Part I, *Studies in Word Association*, Jung demonstrated the autonomy of the complex.

WINTER 1952

Küsnacht, 14th January 1952

Breakfast with C.G. and Mrs. Jung, and a walk afterwards with C.G. He spoke of communists as people without ideals, with whom you could never make a treaty; the peace talks were all nonsense, to wear out the Americans. You can't make peace with termites, they just go on and on; that's how it is with the Russians and it's best to realise it. It is constant attrition, and there's no end to it.

He is working on a manuscript with Marie-Louise von Franz. It is an old manuscript he found in the British Museum and there are copies; one was in Leyden for safety during the War. She is writing a commentary on it, and it will be published as a companion volume to his own writing.[1]

He told me how when he built his house here forty-three years ago, there were meadows all round; the road was quiet and about twice the width of the drive up to the house. His hedge had been at the kerb of the present sidepath and when the road was widened he had to give up part of his garden. We went along to a little park and sat in a shelter – pretty cold, but sunny.

In the evening, after my lecture and dinner later with friends, I returned to Küsnacht at 10.15. Mrs. Jung let me in and said they were in the library. There was C.G. in his usual chair by the window under the lamp. He looked rather older and a bit tired, but he was full of life and, as always, went on to some topic. He wanted to know how many petitions there were in the Lord's Prayer, because he was writing of this (I think correcting galley proofs of his book on Job).[2] I said they were really requests or statements rather than petitions, and he agreed that *requests* was the right word. 'Give us this day our daily bread', not just ordinary bread but the thing we live by. He preferred Jerome's rendering.[3] And he spoke of the wonderful language of the

English translation of the Bible,[4] and also of the Zürich Bible, an excellent translation. He showed me the papal pronouncement,[5] which is in all languages as well as in seventeenth-century baroque Latin; he said I should get a copy as it is immensely interesting.

It was quite a striking picture – C.G. with grey hair and feet up on a chair discussing the type of Latin, and Mrs. Jung behind, a sad look on her face at times.

15th January 1952

Walk in the morning with C.G. – got onto the unconscious. At breakfast he had said how valuable patients' pictures were because they gave us knowledge of the unconscious which was not direct. We can't look at the unconscious directly, it absorbs us. It's like the legend of Perseus who cut off the Gorgon's head: he could not look at it and could not cut it off unless he did, so he used his shield as a mirror. Guided by the reflection in a sideways manner, he wielded his diamond-edged sword and smote off Medusa's head.

Primitives, he said, are in the unconscious all the time. In Africa, with the natives on Mount Elgon, he had to express himself very dramatically to get them to the point of action when he wanted them to do anything.[6]

He spoke of the three principles in science – time, space and causality – and the need for a fourth, namely *synchronicity*. It is a principle. The book he has been writing with a physicist on these things is not yet published.

He mentioned his correspondence, it was 'too much', he would have to give it all his time if he were to attend to it properly.

16th January 1952

Walk after breakfast with C.G. Sunny. He told me again, but in a different way than formerly, his dream of the mediaeval house, as follows:

I am on the first floor of a house, furnished a bit like my study – a sort of eighteenth century type. Now I must see what is downstairs. Beautiful old staircase, and the ground floor is sixteenth century – old, heavy, but beautiful furniture. I thought, 'This is nice, I didn't know it was here – perhaps there is a cellar.' And there was. I went down – bare walls, the plaster coming off, and behind were Roman bricks; a stone flagged floor at the bottom. In one corner was a stone with a ring in it. I lifted it and looked down, and below were prehistoric remains – bones, skulls and old pottery.[7]

He had this dream during his visit to Clark University in America with Freud. He told the dream to Freud who said it must mean he wanted to get rid of someone. Freud kept pressing this point and then said, 'Well, it must mean you want to get rid of your wife.' In their discussion Freud disregarded everything in the dream except the bones and skulls, which he related to the death of someone. He saw the dream only from the point of view of his theory.[8]

Freud was bound up in his theory, it was protective; everything must be reduced to something derogatory, then you were in a superior position. So with spirituality – to Freud it was nothing but sexuality. For him everything could be explained. He asked Jung to promise: 'Promise me that you will support the dogma of sexuality. If we have no dogma, then the black flood of occultism will sweep in and swallow us.'

The Freudians are all suffering from *folie à deux* and reduce everything to something else. As against this is Jung's notion of the collective unconscious, something bigger and greater existing in its own right.

Sitting in the shelter he told me as he finished recounting the dream of the mediaeval house, 'It was then, at that moment, I got the idea of the collective unconscious.'

He said he had had a dream over and over again, before 1930, of a new wing in his house, a lovely room full of wonderful manuscripts. He could make nothing of this then, but when he began to study alchemy he found that it had all been foreshadowed in this recurring dream.[9] He said it was always like this with his dreams; he would dream of what he would write – like the mediaeval house dream and the notion of the collective unconscious.

17th January 1952
We talked of dreams and organic disease, and he spoke of a girl with muscular atrophy. He was consulted and asked for her dreams. She had two: in one her mother was hanging – had hanged herself – from the candelabra in the centre of the room and was swinging there. In

the second dream a horse had gone mad and was in the house; it rushed along the corridor and jumped out of the window.

The mother, the source of life, and the horse, the life principle. C.G. felt, therefore, that the outlook was bad. He said she was not neurotic, she had the disease and the prognosis was grave. Sure enough, she died.

In the case of a man, an American he was seeing, a similar situation evolved. This man dreamt of his father dying, and that meant himself –'I and my Father are one'. Then one day he complained of his throat – some pain or tightness. C.G. thought it could be his heart. He examined the man's heart himself and then sent him to a cardiac specialist who said there was nothing wrong. C.G. wasn't satisfied; he said that as he had sent the patient the specialist had probably thought, 'Oh, it's one of those neurotics!' He sent the patient back for a second consultation telling him that if the specialist found his heart was sound he should get him to state it in writing, and he did so. On the way home after this consultation, with the letter in his pocket saying that there was nothing wrong with him, the man fell dead. He had an aortic aneurysm and the specialist had missed it.

Yesterday C.G. spoke of the Oedipus complex, that Freud had misunderstood it. Oedipus did not know who it was when he killed his father; he was just a man he met. This whole dogma was built on a misunderstanding.

It had been snowing in the night and the sun was shining this morning when we went for a walk, but it was cold. C.G. wore his fur cap. And then the snow came on again.

This afternoon we had five students at the Jung's house. They came, at their request, to discuss case material with me. Before the meeting C.G. met them in his library and chatted for a few moments. Then we gathered for the discussion and Mrs. Jung came in and joined the group. Shortly after C.G. came in also. So I found myself conducting a seminar with, as audience, C.G., his wife, and five students. C.G. did not remain throughout but left after half an hour having contributed to the discussion about my patient's pictures.

At dinner we talked of it all and of other cases. Of one patient he said, 'Let him alone and see what the unconscious has to say,' adding, 'Often I've been very glad that I haven't acted as the saviour.'

Freudian psychology is neurotic psychology. It is based on patients, and patients like the idea that someone has a theory which explains their troubles.

You never think in somatic disease about its cause *only*, you have to deal with it in the present. It's no help just to search for causes and then blame the parents. Why not have the parents as the patients?

Freud's doctrine of resistance: he said of C.G. when he opposed him, 'That's only resistance.' But it might be another point of view; if we persist on and on that it is *only* resistance people get exhausted and may give up their neurosis. But the neurosis shows fight, it's a good thing. At times C.G. has had to re-create a neurosis in order to get vitality into the treatment – for instance when a patient is just flat and deflated.

I raised the question of projections. He said, 'Well, they always appear, and we must expect them. The physician is in the situation and must be prepared to be hurt; if no disease, no health; if no sin, no goodness.'

He mentioned a patient who could not talk, and he said, 'What's wrong with you? Why don't you say what you've come to say?' She asked for a mirror and looked at herself in it, and then added that before seeing him she always looked in the mirror in the waiting room. She was dissociated and had to do this in order to know where she was.

When people talk continuously in a stream it is because they don't want to come to the point, and he may just let them go on. Once with such a patient he fell asleep and had a dream while she was talking; the patient did not notice, and he told her. She remarked, 'Oh, really!' and at once resumed her monologue. 'It's amazing,' said C.G., 'how auto-erotic some people are.'

The psychology of the Jew is bound up with his intellectual capacities and the other side, his instincts, suffer. He illustrated this comment with the story of a Rabbi and his pupils. The Rabbi was teaching, and the pupils agreed with everything he said. Then he stated, 'A barking dog never bites,' and they assented. Soon after they came to a farm and the dog ran out barking at them. At once the Rabbi gathered up his skirts and, with his students, ran into a wood. 'But,' they said, 'you told us a barking dog never bites, why did you run away?' 'Well,' he replied, 'it's quite true, but the dog might not know it.' 'So if you have a theory you must disregard everything else!' added C.G.

At breakfast he spoke of astrology (one of his daughters is interested in it), and of a German book in which he is criticised for giving support to horoscopes. One author wrote to him saying it could not be proved, it was all nonsense; and he had replied, 'But I have always known this.' He went on, 'It's like "bringing owls to Athens", what is the sense in telling me it can't be proved? Of course it can't! What I want to know is *why it works*, for it is amazing how useful it can be. Like the *I Ching*, it's all nonsense if you like; but then it can be absolutely relevant – how is that? Naturally we can't always *prove* things. But there may be some other sort of truth; and *it may be true on a basis we don't know of*. So if we are reasonable we say we don't know how it works; but it can certainly give astonishing insight into character.'[10]

Doctors pay no attention to the mind, to the soul. *Nor does the Church* – we have all got to be miserable sinners and get rid of ourselves and accept a dogma which will save us.

He spoke of psychology as a branch of natural science or medicine. The physician for internal diseases must learn and know what happens when food goes into the stomach. Likewise with the mind, it was precisely the same. Hence his question at the seminar yesterday when discussing my patient's pictures: 'What would you expect the unconscious to be doing in these pictures, having heard the case history of dissociation?' The answer: to produce a compensation, and that is what we find in the first picture and in the others. There is bound to be a reaction.[11] We get patients to draw pictures in order to release something, to let us see what is going on, what the unconscious is doing.

REFERENCES

1 *Aurora Consurgens: A Document Attributed to Thomas Aquinas on the Problem of the Opposites in Alchemy*, edited, with a Commentary, by Marie-Louise von Franz: a companion work to C. G. Jung, *Mysterium Coniunctionis*, CW Vol. 14.

2 C. G. Jung, *Answer to Job*, first published in English in 1954; see also *Psychology and Religion*, CW Vol. 11, VI. The sixth and seventh petitions of the Lord's Prayer are mentioned in Chapter VIII.

3 *C. G. Jung: Letters*, Vol. 2. Writing to Frau Cécile Ines Loos on 7 September

1954 about the petition for daily bread, Jung says: '... in Matthew 6:11 it reads: *"Panem nostrum supersubstantialis da nobis hodie"* (Give us this day our super-substantial bread). At least that is how St. Jerome translated the Greek word, which occurs only in Matthew. ...'

4   The Authorised Version of the Bible.

5   The declaration of the Assumption of the Virgin Mary.

6   These remarks are amplified in Jung's description of his experiences and impressions in Africa in *Memories, Dreams, Reflections*, pp. 238ff.

　　See also Barbara Hannah's account and comments in *Jung: His Life and Work*, pp. 170–78.

7   E. A. Bennet, *What Jung Really Said*, p. 73, the dream is quoted with a footnote: 'Jung mentioned this dream to me in 1951 and in 1961 it was published (E. A. Bennet, *C. G. Jung*, pp. 86, 87). Jung read the book in typescript and added his comments, including one or two verbal alterations. For instance, he added the words, "in *my* house", and remarked that this was of special importance because it showed that he felt identified with the house, it represented the external aspect of the personality, the side seen by others. But in the dream the interior of the house was not familiar. An account of the dream was published again in 1963 [in Jung's *Memories, Dreams, Reflections*, p. 155]. While the wording is not identical with the account just given, the meaning is the same.'

8   These remarks are understood in a wider context if compared with Jung's comments on the dream in *Man and His Symbols*, pp. 56–58.

9   C. G. Jung, *Memories, Dreams, Reflections*, Chapter VII, 'The Work', p. 194.

　　Marie-Louise von Franz, *C. G. Jung, His Myth in Our Time*, Chapter X, 'Mercurius', p. 202.

10 C. G. Jung, *The Spirit in Man, Art, and Literature*, CW Vol. 15, III, *Richard Wilhelm: In Memoriam*, para. 82: 'The fact that it is possible to reconstruct a person's character fairly accurately from his birth data shows the relative validity of astrology. It must be remembered, however, that the birth data are in no way dependent on the actual astronomical constellations, but are based on an arbitrary, purely conceptual time system. Owing to the precession of the equinoxes ... the astrological zodiac on which horoscopes are calculated no longer corresponds to the heavenly one. If there are any astrological diagnoses of character that are in fact correct, this is due not to the influence of the stars but to our own hypothetical time qualities. In other words, whatever is born or done at this particular moment of time has the quality of this moment of time.'

11 The lectures Dr. Bennet gave at the C. G. Jung Institute in Zürich during this visit were later published in *Studien zur Analytischen Psychologie C. G. Jungs*, the *Festschrift* presented to Jung on the occasion of his eightieth birthday in 1955. The chapter is entitled 'The Double', Vol. I, pp. 384ff.

Küsnacht, 21st January 1955
Arrived at Zürich station at 4.30 p.m. and was met by C.G. and Mrs. Jung. To Küsnacht, and a chat with C.G. till dinner. I spoke of spiritual healing, and he mentioned a case of cancer that 'should' have died and seemed hopeless, but the disease didn't develop apparently.

On to *hypnosis*. I asked if Freud gave it up because he could not hypnotise obsessional patients and C.G. said he did not think so; he thought it was because Freud had an enquiring mind and disliked (as C.G. himself did) working in the dark, and so he went on to analysis.

C.G. said he had used hypnotism a lot at one time, and was made to use it by his chief.[1] But he could not get the results others claimed, for example old Forel[2] who described the various stages of hypnosis. C.G. met him through a young colleague who lived near Forel (who had then retired) and asked how he tested the depth of hypnosis. Forel was indignant: 'Test? – why that would be dreadful – you can't waken or disturb hypnotised people by "testing" the depth!' That is, Forel had not tested them but just guessed.

Forel used to hypnotise the old *concierge* at the Burghölzli, and C.G. talked with this man who told him he was never hypnotised. Actually he was and didn't realise it.

Another instance of the same thing was C.G.'s mother. She remarked to him that hypnosis was a lot of nonsense and he replied, 'Oh no, I'll show you.' He told her to hold up her arm, and then said, 'Now you can't put it down.' She said, 'Oh yes I can.' 'Well, put it down then,' said C.G. 'No,' she answered, 'I'm not hypnotised but I don't want to put it down.' Mrs. Jung and C.G.'s sister were there and they laughed. Then he lifted his mother's leg and held it horizontally, and there she sat with her arm up and her leg stuck out. She couldn't move until he told her to do so, and yet she insisted that she was not hypnotised.

Old Forel used to get a group of patients together in a room and tell them to sleep. They would all go off (or pretend to do so) and then he would leave them for a while, and when they heard him returning they would pretend to be asleep again. C.G. said that in Bernheim's clinic at Nancy[3] a gong used to sound when he arrived, and the patients would go off to sleep at once.

The snag about hypnotism is that you remove the initiative from the patient, and this is a bit like [Freudian] psychoanalysis.

It's very important *not* to know all the answers. Often we don't know, and if we did it would be no good, for it is of greater value to the patient when he discovers the answers himself. Patients must not be dependent on the doctor for that weakens them. In a consultation people should be regarded as normal and met socially – their neurosis or problem has to be considered, but it is not the whole of their situation. When people constantly find something wrong with others it means they are undeveloped and project their own inferior side. Jealousy always means that we see someone else doing what we should have done but for our incapacity or laziness; it is easier to criticise other people.

He said how many are impressed by the importance of time, place and causality. But often situations arise where this point of view does not fit in, for instance a prophetic dream – it may be written down and then, perhaps weeks later, the scene appears in real life. Is that causality? Many instances of *déjà vu* are explained in this way.

22nd January 1955

Talk after lunch about *Job*[4] and the reactions to it, the people who appreciated it. He instanced a remarkable letter from a Mother Superior in the Black Forest; it was just like a letter of the thirteenth century – that it had been of such value regarding the Blessed Mother, to know that it was God's idea. Adverse criticisms are numerous. He added that he never has had good reviews; but, like Schopenhauer, 'People read me, and people will read me. I know,' he said, 'because I know what my publisher tells me.'

23rd January 1955

Talk with C.G. after breakfast and we walked to the park. He spoke again of his published work, and about synchronicity.[5] The scientists cannot see it; yet it is so simple. The average is a statistical truth, and this is a concept; but it implies that *there must be exceptions*, and there are exceptions to the general rule of space, time and causality. Some acausal occurrences have the character not of haphazard chance grouping, but of meaningful coincidence, and these he has called *synchronistic events*. He mentioned a man of limited outlook who got a statistician to examine his (C.G.'s) writing on synchronicity; he said it was not sound, and referred to statistical truth. This man also asked C.G. if he believed in astrology because he had mentioned it; but, said C.G., it is not necessary to 'believe' in such concepts – he simply observes that they are sometimes relevant. Scientists speak of *normality* as a statistical truth; but this assumes the inclusion in their concept of things at the extremes which are not 'normal'. He gave an example of measuring all the stones in a square yard of a river bed and taking their average size – say, six inches. That, then, is what stones 'normally' are. But many are bigger or smaller – they cannot be 'normal'. So it is with things outside the conception of space, time and causality; for example precognition, or a dream of a coming event, these are disregarded.

I asked about his visit to Bremen with Freud, prior to their trip to the U.S.A. Freud was upset because Jung wanted to see certain dead bodies which were preserved in the lead cellars (that is cellars where sheets of lead for the church roof were kept), and also other bodies preserved in the soil. Freud thought (and said) 'You want me to die.' He took things personally. Freud fainted on that occasion, at lunch, just after they had talked of these dead bodies, which disturbed him. He fainted again in Munich, and this latter event is the one to which Jones refers.[6] C.G. said that Jones would not know that he and Freud were speaking of Amenophis IV[7] as at that time Jones did not speak German, or at any rate he himself had never spoken to him in German. Jones also came to Clark University and attended the lectures given there by Freud and Jung.

I told him I had resigned from the Society of Analytical Psychology because of power pressures. He said he had done exactly the same thing at the Club[8] years ago; he was out for eighteen months, and they came 'crawling' to get him back again. He said I was abso-

43

lutely right, I could have done nothing else; there were always petty people out for their own ends. ... He went on to speak of how very often people just don't see what they are doing, and said how Germans, even today, blame England for the war because, they say, England did not attack them, and had she done so they would have stopped. He told me of a man who had watched all day at a Rhine bridge for the English planes when the outbreak of war seemed imminent, and when they did not come said, 'Now we can go!' It was like naughty boys looking for some justification for what they are about to do. So in their own eyes the Germans are blameless because they would have stopped if the English had started the fighting! When they are asked about the prison camps they say they knew nothing of them. It's such a big place, Germany, and everything becomes impersonal.

24th January 1955
Drive with C.G. to Greifensee, and on in a circle to Rapperswil along the other side of the lake. At Greifensee, the first village we stopped at, we looked at the outside of an old castle; then we drove on to a Roman castle at Uster which had been restored. It was very cold, but C.G. wasn't tired and pointed out things of special interest. He described how the Romans chose the site where they intended to build, and first ploughed a circle around it; in the centre of this circle they dug a hole, *fundus*, in which they offered sacrifice to the gods of the ground before they began to construct the fortress.

At Rapperswil we walked round the outside of the monastery which is Franciscan. I asked of Father Robertus, the healer of animals. C.G. knew all about him but had never met him; he is now dead. He told me how he had once cured a little sick elephant. A circus – a very famous one – always hibernates in Rapperswil, and among the animals was this little elephant, two or three years old, which fell ill. It did not respond to the treatment given by the local veterinary surgeon; other vets were sent for, still to no avail, and general concern grew as the elephant grew weaker. Eventually, after vets from all over Switzerland had failed to do any good, they sent for Father Robertus. He spent an hour and a half with the elephant, looked into its eyes and stroked it. 'No,' he said, 'it won't come back yet, it's not responsive.' He kept looking into its eyes, stroking it and whispering into its ears; C.G. added in an aside, 'It's always better to whisper to animals.' Finally, after looking at it again Robertus said, 'Now it will get better.' And it did.[9]

The people in that part of the country are mostly Protestant, but they go to the Catholic monastery to get their sick animals healed because their own parsons have 'no more any magic'. The Franciscans have a tradition about the brotherhood of men and animals, and the peasants come to the monks if their cows are 'bewitched'–that is, sick and not giving milk, or not enough. The peasant gives the monk a 5 franc piece –'For,' added C.G., 'even the pious Franciscan monks must live'– and the monk gets him to write the name of the cow on a piece of paper. The peasants think highly of their cows and give them most attractive names; the most beautiful is always Venus. The monk puts the slip of paper in his sleeve, and after a time he will say, 'All right, your cow will give milk tomorrow', and *it does*. The monastery at Rapperswil is famous for its cure of animals.

I asked him how he thought it worked, how the cure came about. He said it was difficult to say, but he thought that at any rate part of it was that when the farmer brought one of his cows to the priest it was quite an occasion, and everybody took it seriously. Consequently the atmosphere in the farm was more tranquil. Cows, he said, were very susceptible to the atmosphere, and if there had been some disturbance or quarrelling at the farm it would upset the supply of milk. In going to the priest all this is overcome, the farmer's mind is set at rest and this helps the cows.

He mentioned that they had a witch doctor at Bollingen, and he also cured cows and was aware of how they reacted in a disturbed atmosphere. Once the witch doctor was consulted when a cow would not give milk and he asked who had milked the cow. The farmer said he had milked it himself but that usually his wife did so. 'Then you must put on a skirt when you milk the cow,' said the witch doctor. The farmer did, and it worked quite well. There was a similar instance when a farmer had electric milkers installed, and the cows, previously milked by women, wouldn't give the milk. The witch doctor's help was sought and he said, 'Get the man who works the electric milker to wear a skirt.' When he did the cows at once gave the full supply; they had been disturbed by the change and were used to women in the shed.

At lunch in the station buffet at Rapperswil C.G. spoke of *active imagination*[10] and of trying unsuccessfully to teach it to a pupil. He told this man he must look at the inner image as a sportsman looks at his target – not to move from it, but let it move. The man had a picture of a steep rocky place and a chamois stood there, quite still. Then the chamois turned its head and gazed at him. He was terrified, jumped out of bed and ran to his wife. There is a part of the mind which moves on its own. This man could not face the unconscious and just ran away. Later he became a Nazi and, like others, was swept into the unconscious, the collective madness of Germany.

I find C.G. very alert and quick in conversation. He is absolutely on the spot, and if something I say isn't clear he questions the point until his understanding is quite precise.

25th January 1955
At breakfast I mentioned dreams, that they are hard to remember. C.G. smilingly said he was the same, 'Perhaps the unconscious just gives up, feels it's no good trying any more!' But he added, 'It's probably because we get set and little alteration is possible or needed.'

We get what we are looking for; if digging for coal we may put uranium on the dump and not see it. So in other things, for instance in the diagnosis of psychiatric conditions.

We talked of group therapy at lunch. He said it has the advantage of dealing with the social factor, this is why he formed the Club in Zürich. But group therapy cannot replace individual therapy, he said; and both men and women should be analysed by someone of the opposite sex, and also by someone of the same sex (for a man cannot constellate the anima fully with a man, nor a woman the animus with a woman).[11] But the social side is needed and individual therapy or analysis cannot supply this.

26th January 1955
Quiet morning, mostly alone.

After lunch, a drive with C.G. and Barbara Hannah, who returned for tea. Dr. Frey came in for dinner and afterwards she and Mrs. Jung went to a meeting in Zürich.

So after dinner C.G. and I go to his study. He, as usual, is in his chair by the window playing patience; he says he likes this because it allows him to assimilate the day – it is possible to play patience and think of something else. I sit by the desk with a shaded light. It is quite silent except for the sound of his cards and my pen writing. ...

Unexpectedly C.G. began to chat about *Job* and described the book to me. The religion of the Old and New Testaments was a cosmogony and, as such, was a psychological matter. (Teilhard de Chardin[12] would not agree.) It – as a cosmogony – showed the *evolving of consciousness out of the unconscious* (good point regarding developmental ideas). Yahweh was an old tribal god and so was cruel, and had to be everything. But his cruelty had to be demonstrated to him: *he needed man to make himself conscious* – man was absolutely necessary. So it was with Christ and the awful blood sacrifice demanded by the Father. 'How is it that no one before has seen it or painted it?' he asked. Then he said, 'It's like the fairy tale, Hans Anderson's,[13] of the rogues who came with a robe for the king, telling him that only those who had never told a lie could see it. The king, having told a lie, could not see it, but could not say so because that would be to give himself away. And in the public gathering no one could see it, nor would anyone admit to not being able to see it until a small boy in his father's arms cried out, "Oh, look at the man in his shirt!" I'm like the little boy,' said C.G., 'for I say what I see.'

People are reading the Bible now, and many did not believe these things were in the Bible, but they are there. It's no good saying that Yahweh is an archaic concept – that's just a psychologism, the very thing people accuse him (C.G.) of making. It's no good, either, saying that he hasn't read the Higher Criticism; he just reads the Bible and if it is not read truly people should be told. Details of the Higher Criticism don't affect the issue for the Bible has not changed for nearly two thousand years. 'I'm sitting in the blue,' he said, 'the doctors won't review or criticise the book, and the theologians can't say what they think!'

He spoke of the Pope[14] as a very able man and said he would like to meet him, but there would not be much point in it as he (C.G.) would not change his point of view and the Pope couldn't. People can't say

C.G. is not a christian because of *Job* because it's all in the Bible, plain to be seen.

He spoke of the Holy Ghost as the spirit of the collective unconscious.

He was in great form and stood in the middle of the floor chatting away in a very animated manner – very difficult to believe he is nearly eighty.

28th January 1955

Walk with C.G. after breakfast. Referring to Father Robertus healing the cows, he spoke of the old practice of a man 'nailing' another and bringing about his death. (*Nailing:* driving a nail into the centre of a tree and thus, gradually, killing the tree and its owner). He said that Riklin (father of Dr. Franz Riklin in Zürich) had told him of a patient who had come to him having 'nailed' his father. The father grew fruit trees, and the son drove a nail into his father's favourite tree, the best he had. Day by day he watched his father going to the tree and looking at the nail, and the son, privately, would give it a further knock each day. In three weeks the father died. The son, oppressed by guilt, came to Riklin as a patient.

He mentioned also that the witch doctor in Bollingen, of whom he had spoken previously, was consulted by a man who was sick. He could not find out why the man was sick, but he discovered that a certain person had 'nailed' him. The witch doctor, who was a big fellow, got this man and made him take him to the tree and pull out the nail. After that the patient got well.

After the walk, a wonderful drive with C.G. We got right above the mist on high ground above Meilen. There we could see the whole range of central Switzerland in the sun and the mist, the sea of mist, below. C.G. pointed out Pilatus, Rigi, Jungfrau, and many other peaks round to the Säntis, also the location of the Lake of Lucerne and Zug and Zürich below in the mist. We could see about sixty or seventy miles and it was quite warm in the sun.

Up there we talked of the old ideas surviving in Switzerland. The *couvade* existed, and may still exist, he said, in French Switzerland; when a woman gives birth while her husband is away, she puts on his military uniform with his sword by her side, so that 'when the devils come they will see that she is protected'. He spoke also of *blood pacts* with the devil up near Bollingen – people would draw blood, and write their name in blood, and so make a pact with the devil. He mentioned a tenant of his who sent to Father Robertus to get his cows cured (as he had previously described). This man's son was the witch doctor at Bollingen, and people came from afar to consult him. Once C.G. asked him if removing the devils affected him, and he said, 'Sure, it does!' He said they used to worry him a lot and made noises in his house – creakings and other sounds. When C.G. asked what he did with the spirits he told him of an old quarry in the woods above Bollingen where he had lodged six hundred devils he had taken from people, and then put a circle (magic) round it so that they couldn't get out. A stranger visiting Bollingen told the girl at the inn that it was so noisy there he would not stay, and she said, 'Oh, but it's perfectly quiet!' Then he told of the creakings and noises in the house he was staying in; C.G. said, 'Isn't that the house where so-and-so lives?' – and it was *the witch doctor's house.*

On returning he pointed out the seventeenth-century building in Küsnacht where Churchill was received.[15] Jung sat beside him representing the 'spiritual and intellectual life of Switzerland'; previously, in Berne, he had had the same honour as the guest of the President of the Confederation, and had been seated beside Churchill's daughter Mary, who had accompanied him. He said Churchill was difficult to talk to unless you got him onto some topic of special interest to him.

C.G. had talked of the Mahdi War[16] in Egypt, and Churchill was quite talkative, and also about politics. He said that Mary Churchill was great fun, quite intoxicated with excitement; flowers nearly filled their carriage, thrown to them, with boxes of cigars. I asked if there was jealousy because he was invited to these two receptions and he said, 'Oh, heavens! I had to hide myself afterwards! But probably I was asked because I know English well and could talk.'

Earlier on the drive he asked if I had finished reading *Job* (I did not know he had noticed that I was reading it) and he asked if I was shocked.

He mentioned asking a professor of theology if he had read the Book of Enoch. The man did not answer directly but said, 'Oh, I must read it!' C.G. said, 'People don't know these things and don't read them.' The term 'Son of Man', he said, came from the Book of Enoch (the authorship of which is unknown), but that it occurred earlier.[17]

He spoke of the end of this Piscean age which is now changing into the Aquarian age, hence the great confusion in our day. He mentioned also the previous age, the Ram, which was worshipped in Egypt; and the age before that, of which we have no clear records, the Bull, in Persia.

He said then that the figure three was masculine, and when the fourth came it was feminine; we had Enoch, Ezekiel and Elijah, and then a fourth, Mary. Similarly, in Egypt there had been three kings and then a fourth – a queen.

After tea I had a chat with Mrs. Jung. I asked about *kinship libido* and she said, 'Yes, it's like the relationship in a family; but also a family relationship should lead to the outer world and is not an end in itself.' Thus while we retained a 'family feeling' for people who came to us for analysis, a friendly feeling, yet it must pass on to the outer world, to collective relationships, relationships outside the family and outside analysis. So also knowledge of the anima should be a stepping-stone to other relationships.

C.G. spoke of his meeting with H. G. Wells in London before the Second War. Wells invited him to dinner and he accepted (I think this was in the late twenties because when C.G. was lecturing in London in 1935 he had a second invitation from Wells which he did not accept). They had a wonderful dinner with champagne, and presently Wells asked him about the origin of a psychosis. In reply he described the mechanisms of schizophrenia and the delusional system; as he talked he was amazed to see H.G.W. 'shrinking'– he seemed to go to nothing in his chair and to be totally concentrated on the conversation, soaking up everything C.G. was saying. Previously he had been very expansive. C.G. talked on telling him a lot, and spoke of projections and the fact that a psychotic person could live out his ideas in life in a way, or try to do so. He talked for about half the evening. When he ended H.G.W. apparently suddenly forgot it all, and was expansive again on completely different topics. All this conversation, with elaborations, came out later in Wells's book, *Christina Alberta's Father*; the whole book, said C.G., hung round that conversation when he watched H.G.W. absorbing it all in a 'most incredible way'. The talk is also reproduced in *The World of Mr. Clissold*, and the evening is recorded in H.G.W.'s autobiography; but he made no mention of what C.G. said, and in neither of the two novels did he make any acknowledgment of him.[18]

In the evening, sitting in the study with C.G. playing patience and Mrs. Jung lying on the couch reading. Very silent and peaceful. I've just finished reading *Job*. It's extraordinary to be in these surroundings with all their associations over the years, and to value them accordingly.

REFERENCES

1 Eugen Bleuler, Professor of Psychiatry in the University of Zürich, and Director of the Burghölzli Hospital when Jung joined his staff in 1900.

2 August Forel, Bleuler's predecessor at the Burghölzli Hospital.

3 During the mid-nineteenth century interest in hypnotic phenomena in France followed the publications of workers such as James Braid. It was Liébeault who, independently, concluded that hypnotic phenomena were purely subjective in origin, and the development of the modern use of hypnotism stemmed from his work. In 1864 he founded what became known as the 'School of Nancy'; he and his followers did not originate a 'school', however, and their views differed widely. Liébeault's work remained obscure until his contribution was recognised in the 1890s by Bernheim, who was then the leading representative of the Nancy 'school'. (*Hypnotism, its History, Practice and Theory*, by J. Milne Bramwell).

4 C. G. Jung, *Answer to Job*, first published in English in 1954. See also *Psychology and Religion*, CW Vol. 11, VI.

5 C. G. Jung and W. Pauli, *The Interpretation of Nature and the Psyche*, first published in English in 1955. Jung's part of this book, 'Synchronicity: An Acausal Connecting Principle', is published also in *The Structure and Dynamics of the Psyche*, CW Vol. 8, VII.

6 Ernest Jones, *Sigmund Freud: Life and Work* (Hogarth Press, London 1955), Vol. II, Chapter V, 'Dissensions', p. 165.

7 The discussion referred to arose over the fact that Amenophis IV defaced his father's tomb, which Freud interpreted as an act which sprang from his negative attitude to his father. Jung pointed out that many pharoahs had altered and re-used the tombs of their forebears for themselves, and that this was an accepted custom; and further, that the defacement consisted in the obliteration of the name 'Amon' for religious reasons. Jung describes the incident and its significance in *Memories, Dreams, Reflections*, Chapter V, 'Sigmund Freud', p. 153.

8 The Psychological Club in Zürich, founded in 1916.

9 Miss Barbara Hannah, in commenting on the cure of the elephant, added that it had been born in the circus and had never known natural freedom. The restric-

tions of the life it led, constantly dominated by men, caused it to sicken and fall ill. It hated men. Father Robertus was the first person to really make contact and communicate with it; in so doing he linked it to men and made the circumstances of life acceptable to the elephant. This is what cured it and enabled it to live.

10   Jung describes the process he termed 'active imagination' in his *Commentary* on *The Secret of the Golden Flower* (translated by Richard Wilhelm and first published in English in 1931), pp. 90–92. The *Commentary* is also published separately, and in *Alchemical Studies*, CW Vol. 13, I, paras. 20–24.

See also C. G. Jung, *The Structure and Dynamics of the Psyche*, CW Vol. 8, 'The Transcendent Function', paras. 167–74.

11   C. G. Jung, *Aion*, CW Vol. 9, Part II, Chapter III, 'The Syzygy: Anima and Animus', para. 42.

12   Pierre Teilhard de Chardin S.J., whose book, *The Phenomenon of Man*, was published posthumously in 1955.

13   Hans Christian Andersen, *The Emperor's New Clothes*.

14   Pope Pius XII.

15   The Haus Schiff in Herrliberg. The reception there, and that in Berne, were held to honour Churchill after the end of the Second War.

16   *Mahdi* is an Arabic title meaning 'he who is guided aright'. According to Moslem tradition, Mohammed declared that one of his descendants would bring equity and justice to the world and would bear the name *al-mahdi*. Through the centuries the title invited the claims of many aspirants, and in 1881 Mahommed Ahmed assumed its authority in his attempt to establish an empire. This was the Mahdist rising of 1884, when General Gordon was sent to Khartum to arrange for the evacuation of the Sudan by the Egyptians. Gordon was besieged in Khartum by the Mahdists, and was killed there in January 1885, two days before his relief force arrived. This was the war referred to here.

17   C. G. Jung, *Psychology and Religion*, CW Vol. 11, VI. *Answer in Job*, paras. 665, 668: The term 'Son of Man' occurs first in Ezekiel, whose writings date from the first half of the sixth century B.C., and it is mentioned once in Daniel (7:13), about 165 B.C. In paras. 677, 678, Jung continues, 'When Yahweh addressed Ezekiel as "Son of Man", this was no more at first than a dark and enigmatic hint. But now it becomes clear: the man Enoch [writing around 100 B.C.] is not only the recipient of divine revelation but is at the same time a participant in the divine drama ... so gripped by it that one could almost suppose he had a quite special understanding of the coming Incarnation.'

18   C. G. Jung, *Alchemical Studies*, CW Vol. 13, I, *Commentary on The Secret of the Golden Flower*, para. 53: 'Insanity is possession by an unconscious content that, as such, is not assimilated to consciousness, nor can it be assimilated since the very existence of such contents is denied. This attitude is equivalent to saying: "We no longer have any fear of God and believe that everything is to be judged by human standards." This hybris or narrowness of consciousness is always the shortest way to the insane asylum. I recommend the excellent account of this problem in H. G. Wells's novel, *Christina Alberta's Father*, and Schreber's *Memoirs of My Nervous Illness*.'

SUMMER 1955

Visit to Zürich on the occasion of C.G.'s eightieth birthday.

Saturday, 23rd July 1955
To Zürich. Met there by C.G., and then to the Seestrasse in Küsnacht for lunch which was followed by the Jung family celebration of his birthday, in which I joined. The celebration was a family boat trip on the *Stafa* from Zürich to Schmerikon; the lake is 43 kilometres long. There were thirty-eight people on board – so many boys and grandchildren; the two little great-grandchildren came to Küsnacht but were too young to come on the boat. Ruth Bailey and myself were the only people present who were not members of the Jung family.

One of the little grandsons stood up completely freely and cheerfully and made a speech to C.G.; he had it typed out and delivered it splendidly. Later we had a quiz, *Fragebogen*, with all the questions about C.G. All the time there were wonderful refreshments, wine, game and fruit *ad lib*.

We alighted at Ufenau, the island near Rapperswil, and went to the church. This island belongs to the monastery at Einsiedeln and they have given C.G. permission to visit it. It is famous as the place where Hutten, a friend of Luther's, spent his last years and died. There are two churches, both old; the larger of the two is Norman, about a thousand years old, but it was closed.

Then we continued up the lake and opposite C.G.'s Tower at Bollingen three of his grandsons dived off the ship from the roof over the deck, quite unexpectedly. The ship swung round and stopped, and they climbed on board again amid cheers. As they dived two fish eagles flew over high up.

Then we went on to Schmerikon, to the *Hotel Bad* where I have stayed on several visits. The host was Herr Kuster, and in the 'cellar', or lower room, a feast was prepared. Upstairs there was a wedding party.

We had a wonderful dinner, interspersed with incidents. To begin with C.G.'s son-in-law, Fritz Baumann, made a speech which evoked great applause; then various groups of grandchildren 'did' items, such as enacting details of the life at Bollingen, and there were plenty of family jokes. Another 'act' was a simulated mixture, or mix–up, of four 'radio programmes': four of the children, two boys and two girls, came and stood in front of C.G. and Mrs. Jung and did a turn. Each was giving, in his or her act, a radio programme; one was on philosophy, one on farming, one (I think) on housekeeping, and one on Analytical Psychology. These 'programmes', of course, got mixed up with amusing complications. Then from the floor, on a large dish, they lifted a huge ham and presented it to C.G. who drew out his familiar pocket knife and cut some slices from it. He always carried this knife. The children did their acts extraordinarily well; they entered into the spirit of it all very naturally and their spontaneity impressed me very much.

Sunday, 24th July 1955
Chat in the morning with C.G. after breakfast. He mentioned the witch doctor at Bollingen, whose house on the hill we had seen from the boat yesterday. The witch doctor has a very ancient book which was given to him by a monk of Einsiedeln who liked him when he was a boy. It is a reprint of an older volume, and contains the so–called sixth and seventh books of Moses.[1] This is a spurious writing which contains black magic and incantations about witches.

The witch doctor *calms people*, and so helps them. C.G. saw him at work once on a farm. The farmer and his two sons stood at the corner of the big barn, and the witch doctor stood at the other. He had his prayer book and read, and he wore a blue ribbon round his neck; C.G. could not get near enough to see what was hung on the ribbon as he had to stay more or less unnoticed at the side.

Monday, 25th July 1955
C.G.J.'s eightieth birthday celebration
There was a reception at 10.30 a.m. in the Dolder Grand Hotel; I

54

went with Barbara Hannah. The notice in the hotel hall was 'Cock-tail Party 10.30'! We had some drinks and the place was crowded with people at little tables. There were speeches by C. A. Meier and others, then the presentation of the *Festschrift*[2] and of the *Codex Jung*,[3] followed by more speeches. The Rector of Basle University spoke, and so did Baūdouin from Lausanne – nice speech. He mentioned the old Swiss custom of erecting a small pine tree decorated with ribbons on a building, when the structure has reached the point when it is possible to put the roof on; then there is a feast. This occasion was like that; Jung's building had gone up to its present height and had taken shape, but it was not yet complete and much may still be added.

We returned for lunch at the Seestrasse, and I chatted with Ruth Bailey in the garden afterwards while C.G. and Mrs. Jung rested.

Later in the afternoon we all talked after tea, sitting round. C.G. was very pleased with the seal I had given him. This was two days ago, and since then he had kept it in his pocket. With it, in the same chamois leather bag, he had a little jade Chinese wishing wheel (it looked eighteenth century and was celadon jade with a movable centre). While we were talking he had the seal in his hand and was looking at it with Mrs. Jung; he said she must get a yellow silk cord to hang it on and pointed out that the stone had been selected because of its dual colour, to carry the idea of the opposites.

In the evening the big dinner was held. About seventy-five people were there. To my great surprise I was placed at C.G.'s right hand at the main table; on my right was his daughter, Mrs. Marianne Niehus. There were ten people at this big round table; Mrs. Jung was there also, with Michael Fordham to her right.

There were several speeches at the dinner, including one from the Mayor of Zürich, and a lot of jokes about the relative merits of Basle and Zürich, and some allusions to Berne.

Wednesday, 26th July 1955
This was C.G.'s actual birthday. We had a meeting in the morning at the Institute[4] regarding the formation of the International Association for Analytical Psychology.

In the afternoon there was a trip on the lake on a chartered steamer;

about two hundred people were there. To everyone's joy and surprise C.G., with Ruth Bailey, joined the ship at Meilen; they left it again at Rapperswil. Many had been sure they had seen C.G. in the garden of his house as the ship passed, but this could not have been the case.

On the return journey I left the ship at Küsnacht (having nearly got left behind on the boat) with a big bunch of flowers and a stick with '80' carved on it for C.G. Meier threw a bottle to me from the deck, which I caught; I chucked it back to Fowler McCormick and he also caught it – great cheers.

I was given a lift to the Jungs' house and on arrival found the local band of Küsnacht playing in the garden. There were about twenty players with the usual instruments, brass and others. As they played some of the family party danced; C.G. danced twice, once with his wife and again with one of his daughters. Later he told me, 'I never thought I would dance again!' He was in great form.

When the band dispersed we went into the house, and for a couple of hours or more there followed the most wonderful evening. Seven or eight of the Jungs' children and grandchildren sang and played; a niece, Frau Homberger, played the piano and her husband sang with the others. Several of the grandsons were very lively, entering into the spirit of the occasion.

Then some left, and C.G. went out and returned with a selection of gramophone records; they were all of negro spirituals. One of his grandsons worked the gramophone and C.G. sat beside it, listening and nodding his head in time with the music. Eventually, at about midnight, the party came to an end; it was a remarkable and impressive family evening.

27th July 1955
In the garden, writing about the birthday proceedings for the *B.M.J.*
    Several talks with C.G. ...
    In the evening Franz Riklin took me to Meilen for the first meeting of the provisional committee of the proposed International Association; this we held in a hotel in Meilen overlooking the lake. There were a few discondant elements which stemmed from the London group, and one or two people took a very negative attitude. Riklin and

Meier were amazed but I was not. Returned to the Jungs' house at
1 a.m., brought by Riklin.

28th July 1955

Moved to the Waldhaus Dolder Hotel. At noon Fowler McCormick
called for me. I was sorry to go for it had been one of the most event-
ful visits to the Jungs I had had. Mrs. Jung said I must certainly stay
with them when I come over to lecture next February; and C.G. also
said warmly, 'Well goodbye, and be sure to come back soon.'

Fowler McCormick took me to Schaffhausen where we had an
excellent lunch and then visited the Rhine falls. He has an Oldsmo-
bile car and we had a lovely drive in sunny weather.

29th July 1955

At the Waldhaus Dolder. Went into town in the morning, shopping;
called at Rolf Hofer's office and got his secretary to type a short article
on Jung for the *B.M.J.*[5] She did this and posted it for the evening air
mail to get to London on Saturday morning. No lunch; but tea with
Fowler McCormick at the Congress House. Wet.

McCormick talked of synchronicity, and then mentioned two of
his dreams in which he had been impressed by the time element for
in both a later event carried the dream further, and it was immediately linked in his mind with the dream. The most striking of these
was a dream in which he saw two aeroplanes weaving a cord (or rope)
in the sky in such a way that they joined Europe and America. He
saw this as a commentary upon his life, divided between the conti-
nents and somehow coming together, for he is constantly passing
from one to the other.

REFERENCES

1 'The five books of Moses' is a description given to the Pentateuch, the first five
books of the Old Testament, traditionally ascribed to Moses.

2 *Studien zur Analytischen Psychologie C. G. Jungs*, Vols. I and II (Rascher,
Zürich 1955).

3 Jung's address at the presentation of the *Jung Codex* is published in *The Symbolic Life*, CW Vol. 18, p. 826. A footnote describes how the *Nag-Hamadi
Gnostic Codex* was purchased from the estate of Albert Eid, a Belgian dealer in
antiquities who had acquired it in Egypt. Jung later returned it to the Coptic

Museum in Cairo (see conversation of 12 January 1961). The *Codex* was published in three volumes: *Evangelium Veritutis* (Rascher, Zürich 1956), dedicated to Jung's eightieth birthday; *De Resurrectione* (Rascher, Zürich 1963); and *Tractatus Tripartitus Pars I* (Francke, Bern 1973).

4 The C. G. Jung Institute in Zürich.

5 E. A. Bennet, 'Carl Gustav Jung at Eighty', *British Medical Journal* (1955), II, p. 174.

AUTUMN 1955

Arrived at Zürich station at 12.25 and was met by C.G. He told me Mrs. Jung was very ill and so I would not be staying with them but with his daughter Marianne Niehus. But he took me to the Seestrasse for lunch; his second daughter, Mrs. Baumann, was there.

We had a long talk after lunch, mainly about schizophrenia. This followed my reference in a lecture to a psychotic patient. He spoke of schizophrenia as a protection from the shadow, and usually the collective shadow. Some say they can't be perfect and recall some episode in the distant past; but they refuse to look at recent events, the sin of yesterday, that is too much for them. Or when people are in a depression they may, on the contrary, take on the sins of the whole world. He also spoke of the Germans who must always be 'behind' something – no confidence in just being a man; they must belong to a society, or be a doctor, or have a title. Even an ordinary person, for instance a woman who has died, is described as 'so-and-so, the wife of ...', not just as herself. In England it is different; being a gentleman is enough, but not in Germany.

He spoke of his wife's illness and his dead friends coming in his dreams – death is in the air. He had a feeling that the bridge had broken, she was different.

Later he mentioned his religious experience at Basle at the age of eleven[1] and went on to talk of his father's library. He himself was a voracious reader and some books from his grandfather's library were there, so he read everything. He said that even at school he had always been suspected of being a fraud – as when the teacher refused to believe he had written his essay; there was so much in it the teacher had never heard of that he concluded C.G. had got someone else to write it for him.[2] 'I was always a bit too intelligent and people didn't like it, thought there was some trick about it.'

27th November 1955

Mrs. Jung died at 10.30 this morning. C.G. came up to the Niehus's house to tell me and to say goodbye. He said that four days ago, on Tuesday at breakfast, she had said she felt she was going to die and he said, 'Oh, don't think of such things'. Later that morning he received the medical report they were awaiting which showed how grave the prognosis was. He struggled with himself about telling her but he did so; she was quite undisturbed, and in a way relieved for ever since her operation she had been preparing for death. Sometimes she had looked better, but she was very 'grey' at other times. She had been working on the Grail legends in the original.[3] They had been married fifty-two years – a very full and wonderful life. He spoke of Cicero's *De Senectute* (that is, 'concerning old age'), and how life ended when it was fulfilled.

REFERENCES

1 C. G. Jung, *Memories, Dreams, Reflections*, Chapter II, 'School Years', p. 47.

2 *Ibid.*, pp. 54 and 72–73.

3 Mrs. Jung's work on the Grail legend, which remained unfinished at the time of her death, was completed by Dr. Marie-Louise von Franz, who writes in the Foreword: 'The connections between the Grail legend and alchemy are so abundant and so profound that it may well be asked why Professor Jung did not include them in his researches into the psychology of alchemy. The reason was that Mrs. Jung had been engaged on the Grail legend for thirty years and was planning an extensive publication on the subject. Her labours were cut short by her death in 1955 when, in response to Professor Jung's wish, I undertook to bring her work to a conclusion.' Emma Jung and Marie-Louise von Franz, *The Grail Legend* (Rascher, Zürich 1960; English translation by Andrea Dykes, The C. G. Jung Foundation 1971).

Küsnacht, 29th August 1956
Arrived in Zürich.

30th August 1956
At breakfast C.G. spoke of the difficulties implicit in the idea of anyone writing his biography; he said it would require a full understanding of his thought, and no one understood it completely. Freud's life,
he said, could be clearly described because his thought was simply
laid out. But with him it was more complex, for unless the development of his thought were central to his biography it would be no more
than a series of incidents, like writing the life of Kant without knowing his work.[1] To illustrate his meaning he mentioned a momentous
dream he had had in 1913. The experience had an important influence upon his life which resulted from the efforts he made to understand the dream; yet were it related quite simply few people would
comprehend the significance it had at that point in his career. The
dream:

He was climbing a steep mountain path, twisting to the top, and on the
right the valley was in shadow for it was still night; ahead the sun was behind the peak and rising, but still hidden. In front of him was a primitive
man (the man of all the ages – brown-skinned and hairy); he was following
this man and each was armed for hunting, probably chamois. Then the sun
rose, and on the summit of the mountain Siegfried appeared in shining ar-
mour with a shield and spear; he was wearing something like skis and glided
down over the rocks. The skis were of bones – the bones of all the dead.
Then the primitive man indicated to him that they must shoot Siegfried
with their rifles, and they lay in wait for him and killed him. The primitive
man (the shadow) was the leader; he went to collect the spoil. But C.G.
was filled with remorse and rushed down the mountain into a ravine and
up the other side – he had to get away from the awful crime. It was raining

and everything was wet; but while this washed away all traces of the crime it made no difference to the sense of guilt which oppressed his conscience.

He awoke and wanted to sleep again but he knew he must try to understand the dream. For a while his remorse for murdering Siegfried – the hero – obliterated everything else, overwhelming him to the extent that he felt impelled to take his revolver from the drawer and shoot himself, 'commit suicide'; the dream and the impulse were terribly vivid and he might have done it but for the fact that his thoughts about the dream began to take shape: the hero, doing the very heroic act, was killed by the primitive man. That is, the dream was pointing to the primitive man, who was immoral or undeveloped in our eyes, as the leader, the one to be followed. For him, this meant that he must follow not the here and now of consciousness, the accepted achievements, but the man of the ages who represented the collective unconscious, the archetypes.

This dream was a big turning point in C.G.'s life – a far more significant dream than that of the mediaeval house, he said. For it showed that he must follow a certain line and disregard popular ideas. It was like the old Austrian saying of never doing today what can be done tomorrow; that is, time is not the important thing. American boys carve on their desks 'Do it now', and this appeals to people today; but to do this, and to say 'Where there's a will there's a way' isn't everything. We must get in touch with the man of the ages, not be over-impressed by the present, not be rushed. In the dream the primitive man behaved naturally, as a primitive man would do – seeing someone approaching with sword and shield, he just fired and killed him. So C.G. knew from the dream, when he came to comprehend it, that he must follow the deep hidden, discarded primitive man, and forsake his academic scientific career, the heroic role of doing things here and now and 'getting on' ('This world's empty glory' E.A.B.).[2]

He mentioned that Freud discovered the first archetype, the incest problem. But he had regarded it only from the personal point of view, just as he took religion as simply a personal matter. As such it could be disregarded. He added that Freud never acquired any idea of the deeper unconscious although he spoke of 'archaic memories'.[3]

C.G. said that in the Oedipus complex lies a great deal of importance; it is the separation of the child and the parents, and the attitude of the child to the parents. I asked if this wasn't the problem in neurosis – the conflict of the personal and the collective; the desire just to be apart, and the difficulty in adapting to the whole, taking one's place in the group. It can show itself in many forms of phobias (claustrophobia etc.) where the underlying fear is of being alone and so faced with the central problem of adjustment. But this varies in different ages; in the first half of life it is personal adjustment to life around us, and in the second half the adjustment is to the bigger spiritual life which goes on and on.

He mentioned Bollingen, that the great thing about it for him is that it is so near to nature. They cook on the open fire there, and he does most of the cooking and cuts the firewood – only wood is used. Speaking of the fire he said, 'We haven't yet mastered the natural forces so you have to know how to use it.'

We strolled round the garden (at Küsnacht) and he pointed out all the trees which had been killed by frost. There had been warm weather in January, and the very severe frost in March burst a lot of the stems of the laurel, wistaria and other trees, because the sap had risen and it froze. The bamboos also had to be cut down but they have shot up again and there is a very fine grove of delicate trees some ten or twelve feet high. A feature of the house is that it was built originally with only one door. C.G. said this was because 'We Swiss live in the centre of Europe and lots of things may happen.' In previous days, at the time of his army service, he had his rifle and thirty rounds of ammunition in the house (all Swiss soldiers have) so that he could defend himself. The lower windows are protected by grilles of steel or bars. The garden room was built later – it has a door to the garden and another into the house; the latter is an iron door and is always closed at night.

C.G. has a doze after lunch and so has Miss Bailey. I sit in the garden, and today it is beautifully sunny.

Later we talked again, and C.G. said how interesting it would be if someone were to study the dreams people had under anaesthetics; he mentioned one or two examples. Also he spoke of his great interest on reading that a neuro-surgeon, concerned with epilepsy, had stimulated the *corpora quadrigemina*[4] and the patient had had a vision of a mandala, a square containing a circle. This vision could be reproduced – and was reproduced – by the stimulation of the same area. He said he had for a long time thought that the brain stem was important in our thinking life and how interested he was that the *corpora quadrigemina*, the four bodies, was the area, for it confirmed his idea of the importance of the square and the circle as symbols.

In the evening after dinner, we somehow got onto the subject of numbers which, C.G. said, had a life of their own. It was always a problem for mathematicians – had numbers been invented or discovered? This cropped up in talking about what *religion* was; was it with Origen, *relegare*: to connect, link back, or with Cicero, *relegere*: to gather up again, to recollect – that is, something that is there already? The latter is C.G.'s idea for in thinking of religion we must think of all religions, for instance Buddhism, which is a religion without a god. But theologians say they are concerned only with Christianity! This is like a doctor saying he is only concerned with viruses and is not interested, for example, in malaria. So in religion we must avoid specialisation, concentrating on one thing only and leaving out the rest because it does not suit us.

Then we passed on to talk of numbers and their individual qualities. *One* was nothing, because you could only think of one if you had a lot of ones; but also it could be Everything, like One (and the Many), that is the totality of God. *Two* was the opposites – good and evil – and was left out by those who did not hold with opposites, such as those who accept the idea of the *privatio boni*. *Three* was the dynamic number; it was male. I said, 'For example, one, two three – go!' and he said, 'Yes, that's it, it's leading somewhere.' *Four* is female, complete; it is an end, final. *Five* is four plus one, but the one is in the centre, it is the quintessence of the four. *Six* is the double three (there was more to this). *Seven*, the divine number, six plus one; the seven branched candlesticks (more also to this). *Eight* – the double four. *Nine* is the double four plus the central one, the quintessence again. C.G. thinks of numbers as things existing in themselves which are discovered, not just invented.[5]

31st August 1956
Talk with C.G. after breakfast about theologians – he found them 'terribly superficial'. They don't mind talking and a lot of their

thought was 'just firing blank ammunition'. But when it comes to real firing – taking things seriously and seeing what they really are, they close up. He mentioned the story of the trumpeter of Schaffhausen. In the eighteen-forties there was fighting in Switzerland between the cantons; the Schaffhausen regiment went to take part and the trumpeter went with them. In a week he reappeared in Schaffhausen and everyone asked, 'Why aren't you at the war?' 'Oh,' he said, 'they aim at you there!'– so he had come home. Theologians are often like that.

Then he went on to talk of the Pope's dogma about the Assumption of the Virgin Mary, and said it had great opposition in the Church because it is laid down that there can be no dogma unless it is founded upon Apostolic teaching, and there was no reference to the ascension of the Virgin until the sixth century. But the Pope overrode that. Several popes had attempted it before; one had done so a hundred years ago but he did not succeed in pushing it through. The whole point of the dogma is to counteract the *material*; yet the woman is *mater* (that is *material*) and God is manifest in creation, in matter. There was tremendous opposition to the dogma, principally in northern countries; but the southern countries pressed for it. The Virgin, therefore, is 99.9999 per cent God – but not quite. What will happen next? The Virgin is now in the Bridal Chamber. I asked if it meant another Christ and he said, 'Oh *no*, there can be only one Son of God.'

Laurens van der Post came for lunch and talked of his African adventures.[6] C.G. spoke also of *participation mystique* – that *everything is known*. The primitive acts in that way; nothing is hidden nor can anything be hidden, it all comes out. C.G. is very keen on this idea, hence the title of his book *Modern Man in Search of a Soul*.

In the evening after dinner C.G. spoke of his first visit to Freud in Vienna.[7] While staying there he had a dream:

He was in the ghetto in Prague and it was narrow, twisted and low-ceilinged, with staircases hanging down. He thought, 'How in hell can people live in such a place?'

That was the dream. He went on to speak of how from the time of their first meetings he had noted the narrowness of Freud's standpoint, his limited perspective and concentration on tiny details. He mentioned that to some degree it was because of Freud's mother-complex that he was so concerned with sexual things – incest, sleeping with the mother and so on – as if they were something new. C.G., having been brought up in the country, knew all these things but they did not interest him. The old ghetto in Prague, he said, was a famous one.

REFERENCES

1 These remarks anticipate Jung's approach in writing his autobiography, *Memories, Dreams, Reflections*, during the last years of his life.

2 C. G. Jung, *Memories, Dreams, Reflections*; the dream, and his reactions to it, are described in the chapter 'Confrontation with the Unconscious', pp. 173–74; relevant also are pp. 185–86.

3 Sigmund Freud, *Moses and Monotheism* (Hogarth Press 1939), p. 159: 'The archaic heritage of mankind includes not only dispositions, but also ideational contents, memory traces of former generations.'

4 The *corpora quadrigemina* are four rounded eminences forming the dorsal part of the mid-brain. They are arranged in pairs: *superior* and *inferior colliculi*; the former are associated with sight, the latter with hearing.

5 C. G. Jung, *The Structure and Dynamics of the Psyche*, CW Vol. 8, VII, *Synchronicity: An Acausal Connecting Principle*. In para. 871 Jung writes of the qualitative concept of number, leading to the statement: 'I incline to the view that numbers were as much found as invented, and that in consequence they possess a relative autonomy analogous to that of the archetypes.'

This is the standpoint from which Dr. Marie-Louise von Franz has written *Number and Time* (Northwestern University Press 1974); in Part I, Chapter 3, p. 52, she writes: '... numbers appear to represent both an attribute of matter and the unconscious foundations of our mental processes. For this reason, number forms, according to Jung, that particular element that unites the realms of matter and psyche. It is "real" in a double sense, as an archetypal image and as a qualitative manifestation in the realm of outer-world experiences. Number therefore throws a bridge across the gap between the physically knowable and the imaginary. In this manner it operates as a still largely unexplored mid-point between myth (the psychic) and reality (the physical), at the same time both quantitative and qualitative, representational *and* irrepresentational.'

6 Laurens van der Post, *The Heart of the Hunter* and *The Lost World of the Kalahari* (Hogarth Press).

7 Jung first met Freud in February 1907. He describes the occasion in *Memories, Dreams, Reflections*, Chapter V, 'Sigmund Freud'.

Küsnacht, 3rd January 1957

Arrived in Küsnacht. In the evening we sat first in the garden room, and after dinner in the library upstairs. This is a big room, about twenty-four feet by fifteen feet, lined with books. Off it opens an inner study, and C.G. told me I could use this as my room for writing. It is a smallish room, and in it I now write at the big table-desk with an array of pigeon holes on it to take stationery and odds and ends. There is a photograph of Toni Wolff on the table, and also a rather beautiful collection of twenty-one figures representing all the states in India; each one is labelled. They depict the different apparel of the peoples of India, and are about ten centimetres in height and delicately made and coloured. The religions also are marked on the labels – Hindu, Buddhist, Islam (Baluchistan), and one from Burma. On a side shelf are two lovely cloisonné pieces, one of a sage on a creature with horse's legs and the head and tail of a dragon; the other is an old vase. On the pigeon-hole part of the desk are books and a few other figures – one a beautifully carved ivory figure of Lao-tse on a stag, the same as the two I have.

There are three lights in the window and an amount of stained glass in the panels. At the top of each segment is a religious subject – Christ being lashed with whips on the left; in the centre, the crucifixion; and on the right our Lord after death with Mary weeping; two disciples are there with Mary Magdalen, and above is an angel. In the centre window below is an elaborate coat of arms dated 1590, and on the right the arms of Basle dated 1543, 'Basilea 1543'. The centre light also contains a small round inset of stained glass showing our Lord and the twelve apostles at the last supper.

One picture is covered with a cloth; it is a photograph of the Shroud of Turin, the cloth which is said to have covered our Lord's face and afterwards bore the imprint of his features.

The walls are lined with bookcases; there are many old alchemical books and books of reference of all kinds. They are labelled and no doubt catalogued; both rooms are filled with them. There are also numerous ornaments of various kinds, many of them gifts. On the mantelpiece in the main study is a collection of little ivory carvings depicting the twelve transitions of Vishnu.

C.G.'s writing table is a beautiful mahogany or walnut table with curved legs and a finely shaped stringer. It is covered with papers and other objects. C.G. told me that one, a metal figure, bearded, and sitting on an elephant, represented a previous incarnation of the Buddha; in Christianity it would correspond to one of the disciples, a special associate of the master. And there is a carved lotus which opens out – a present from the Indian Psychiatric Society. In a standing bookcase are some small leather-bound books; and there is a photograph of Mrs. Jung, and another of C.G. with her. On the floor of the main study, as in the inner room, are a couple of Persian rugs. All the floors in the house, the rooms and the landings, are parquet.

4th January 1957
Speaking of his early work at the Burghölzli, C.G. said that when his observations on the word association tests were established he wrote to Freud telling him how these experiments provided clinical proof of his theory of repression. He said, too, that he had noted that the complex acted autonomously, and apart from repression. Although in his reply Freud agreed with this, he never made use of the idea of unconscious autonomy and confined his interest to the phenomenon of repression.

Besides his work on the word association tests, Eugen Bleuler, his senior at the Burghölzli, suggested that C.G. should do research on the brain. He turned to this with enthusiasm, working many hours week after week on the various parts of the brain. He became keen on the work and used to deputise for the Professor and give lectures on histology. But so far as the normal functioning of the mind was concerned, or abnormalities in thinking which he observed in patients, this work on the histology of the brain was fruitless.

Many of the patients in the hospital were schizophrenics and no attempt was made to treat them. But he could not accept *dementia praecox* as deterioration of the personality and leave it there. Through the word association tests he had come to see the reality of the unconscious, and he recognised that many of the fantasies or delusions of his patients were paralleled in mythological material of which they knew nothing. *The Psychology of the Unconscious*[1] was a study in schizophrenia; in it he showed the significance of symbols through historical and literary analogies. But the book was not a psychological study; one of the difficulties in those days was that there was no psychology, only intellectual abstractions which explained nothing. People paid little attention to what might lie behind the symptomatology of an illness. *The Psychology of Dementia Praecox*[2] was an advance, but even now psychiatrists have paid little tribute to it. *The Relations between the Ego and the Unconscious*[3] was written to bring people into touch with the unconscious and make them aware of its importance, but it, too, made very little impression.

During the First War he was in command of a camp on Lake Geneva at Château-d'Oex for interned British and Canadian officers. He said that for some this would have been important and interesting work, but he was more concerned with his writing and the development of his thought. He was then working on *Psychological Types*.[4]

I asked him if, looking back, he could see a single thread running through his work. He said only to a certain extent. In the early days he had expected his work to follow scientific lines. But after the break with Freud he did no scientific work for a time, but sought to discover the meaning of the contents of the unconscious. To discover where ideas came from, and how others understood them in the past, he searched for the historical and cultural sources of the images and symbolism he encountered. It was when he had written his commentary on *The Secret of the Golden Flower* that he began to study the writings of alchemists and found links with this material through parallels in the imagery of their thought and practices, and through their understanding and interpretation of ideas from still earlier times. His study of alchemy had been foreshadowed in his dreams, and his work had always developed in this way – out of his own experiences and dreams. He mentioned by way of illustration a dream he had in April 1914; with variations it recurred twice, once in each succeeding month:

He was climbing up the hill above Küsnacht to the plateau where now the Niehuses[5] have their house. But it took nearly all day and in fact the hill is not very high. He got to the plateau just as the sun was setting behind him (it does set on the hills on the opposite side of the Zürich Lake). A cascade of water was falling down the hill, and the sun lit it up with silver and gold. Away to the left, and higher up – for there was another hill behind, though not so high as the one he had ascended – he observed a big hotel (such as the Dolder Hotel), and he could see the cars parked there looking very small.

He could not understand the dream then. But much later he discovered an alchemical text, *Speculativa Philosophia (Theatrum Chemicum (1602), I)* of Gerald Dorn, in which a similar scene was described. The gold and silver in the water had a special meaning, and the building was there as well; it was not a hotel, as in his dream, but a building of great symbolic importance.[6]

Dreams such as this fascinated him. 'That's the worst of being an introvert,' he said, 'you are pushed on by your inner drives.'

He said that Freud was really a feeling type, but he kept this back and worked with his inferior thinking, so what he thought had too great a significance for him. It even came about that he believed things were so merely because he had thought them.

He mentioned the notion of pre-vision, that sometimes it was like a waking dream. On one occasion he was sitting at Küsnacht reading the paper, and suddenly there was a gap in it, a big hole, in which he saw the face of Hans, the servant at Bollingen. (This youth was devoted to C.G., for during the war C.G. had given food to his mother, who was poor with several children, and he had bought a bicycle for Hans so that he could go to school). Shortly after, to C.G.'s great surprise, Hans arrived in the garden at Küsnacht. C.G. had no idea he was coming but he had cycled from Bollingen (about 37 kilometres) to bring C.G. some early strawberries.

He told me of another incident, during the Second War when petrol was scarce. He was returning to Küsnacht from Bollingen by train and was reading, but his mind became insistently occupied with the idea of a man being drowned – something he had once seen. Why should he think of it now? But he could not get the thought out of his mind. When he reached his house in Küsnacht some of his grandsons (who were living there at the time) were in the garden looking rather upset, and he asked, 'What's up? What's the matter?' They told him the youngest boy, who could not swim, had fallen into the water in the boat-house; it is very deep there and they had had great difficulty in getting him out. C.G. said, 'That would have been about half an hour ago?'– the time when the idea of drowning had filled his mind in the train – and they said, 'Yes, that was the time.'[7]

5th January 1957

I asked C.G. if he had ever, as it were, heard the future calling him. He said it was never like that with him. He knew others – Goethe, for example – had felt that; but for him it was always something behind, a *vis a tergo*, pushing him on to find the truth, what things really were. He had never been satisfied with Freud's theory because it lacked historical support; it had no background, it was no more than Freud's theory. Yet, he said, it was to Freud's credit that he tried to find a background in *Totem and Taboo*.[8]

It was after he had written *The Relations between the Ego and the Unconscious* that C.G. became interested in Chinese thought. In 1928 he had a letter from Richard Wilhelm asking if he would write a commentary on *The Secret of the Golden Flower*[9], a book on Chinese alchemy, and he did so. He found Chinese thought impressive and studied the *I Ching*. Through his study of types C.G. found similarities with Chinese thought; he drew a diagram of the four functions to illustrate what he meant:

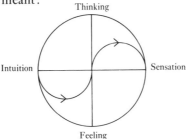

Thus if a man is predominantly a thinking type he begins to speculate; so he takes in intuition, the knowledge from the unconscious. But he wants then to see how it relates to facts, and so sensation is included. This results in a triangle which excludes feeling. This happened, he said, with Freud. But the feeling is there, nevertheless. 'I had a hell of a lot of trouble with that!' said C.G. When feeling is left out you get a narrow circle round the thinking, the intellectual function. But, he observed, the diagram of the functions corresponds to the Yin Yang of the Chinese, it makes for completeness.

I gave him the synopses of my lectures to read and he expanded on parts of them and said he thought they did give the bones on which the flesh could be put. He digressed a good deal and all he said was interesting.

When he came to *free associations* he said they were futile for they lead only to the complexes; but in dream-analysis they do not tell us what the dream says. He gave an example: 'Think of a man who dreams of a daisy and you ask for his associations; he says, "Well, Daisy is a name, it's the name of my girl friend." Freud would go on from there to sex. But I would say, "That's interesting, but what about the daisy? It's still there on the ground – what of the daisy itself?" Then the man might say, "Well, it's a flower with white petals and a golden centre; it draws health from the sun and opens when the sun shines. It exists in itself, apart from other daisies." So then I ask, "What about the sun?" and he may think of God or religion. But that is not Daisy, his girl friend. So *the unconscious is producing something* which shows that there is more than Daisy, there is his own life and also a greater life.'

The Self – it is the whole, conscious and unconscious, 'what I myself am'; it involves much we do not know is there, for example our body and its workings, and the unconscious.

6th January 1957
In the morning C.G., Ruth Bailey and I went up to Bollingen by car. The sun was shining and the place looked wonderful with the new room added, and the painted ceiling in the loggia. The painting of this ceiling was C.G.'s idea; his coat of arms, or the separate parts of it, fill a long panel at one end and at the other end is that of Mrs. Jung. The intermediate panels are painted with the crest of the Hoernis (one of their daughters married into this family) – the emblems were horns, hunting horns. Opposite this is the Baumann crest (another daughter married one of them). That of the Niehus family (their

other son-in-law) was not yet complete and there was a space. In the two centre panels the crests of C.G. and Mrs. Jung were repeated.

We went up to the new room. The woodwork and metal work of the door hinges and door knobs was excellent and C.G. said it was old.

He told me about the original building, and of the various additions as time went on. We looked at some of the many stone carvings he has done; a small one was of a snake which had swallowed a perch and died. A beautiful stone in the classical style was a memorial to Mrs. Jung; this, he said, was to be put up on the wall by the loggia. At the side of the house is a carving of Mercury. I asked why he had done it. He said that when he was writing on synchronicity something restricted him – he just could not get it right. His eye kept looking at the stone wall at the side of the tower, and he decided to fixate (my word) the interruption and carved a rather smiling face depicting Mercury; beneath he inscribed the words: '*O* (that is, Mercury) *Fugaci illi. Ambiguo, duplici, illudendi jocoso*'. That did it. He could then get on with his work.[10]

On our return we passed the old church between Rapperswil and Bollingen. C.G. said it dated back to the seventh century and had frescoes of the fifteenth century. It was dedicated to Dionysius the Areopagite,[11] and no churches were dedicated to him after the eighth century.

After coffee on the verandah, following lunch, C.G., Ruth and I went and sat on the pier by the lake and fed the swans; nine of them collected and seagulls came. The seagulls breed on the upper lake and remain here all the time. There were also some coots. It was sunny and when C.G. went for his sleep, I sat on a chair by the lake in the shelter of the pier; it was beautifully warm.

Later I talked with C.G. in the garden room while he sat in front of the stone he was working on and now and then chipped at it.

He spoke of the importance of rumours as psychological phenomena, and in particular of those concerning flying saucers. That there are such rumours, so widespread, is significant. A fact which impressed him in one case was that the radar beam had been deflected; this is beyond rumour and remains a most important, though unexplained, fact. There seems to be something factual about the hundreds of well-attested reports over many years of these phenomena.

A Californian psychiatrist was driving over a bridge in San Francisco with his wife when she suddenly saw these things in the sky and called his attention to them. He glanced at them, but as he was driving could do no more. C.G. heard of the incident and wrote to him; he replied saying he had seen the objects but was puzzled to know why C.G. should be interested in such things. C.G. was amazed that this man could be so wooden-headed as to disregard such a phenomenon. He said it was certain that these things could not be explained by our ordinary categories of thought; we had to take note of them for they may well come from outside our world, as we know it. The French have a special bureau to investigate them, and so have the Americans.

He referred also to the remarkable effect of an American broadcast (this was Orson Welles's radio adaptation of H. G. Wells's *The War of the Worlds*) about an invasion of New York by people from Mars. People were ready to accept this, as though they were inwardly expecting some momentous event from outside.

In the 'little room', that is the inner study in which I write, and on the table-desk, is the cricket ball presented to C.G. by the Society of Analytical Psychology in London with the inscription: 'The C. G. Jung Anniversary Cricket Match 10.7.55'. This was presented to C.G. by Dr. Leopold Stein on behalf of the S.A.P. at the birthday party dinner at the Dolder Hotel in Zürich 1955.

C.G. enjoys detective stories, and I asked him why. He turned the question and asked me what I thought. I suggested that people like to identify themselves with, for instance, the clever detective; or in the story they find a character doing all the things they would like to do if they dared. He said this was probably true, but his own interest was that the stories had nothing to do with him or his work; most of them, too, were about men. Many novels had psychological themes and these bored him for he had plenty of this with his patients, far more interesting stuff. But the detective stories were a rest, chiefly because they had no bearing on his professional work; and he could sleep after reading them because they were not true.

7th January 1957

In the afternoon we sat in the garden room; C.G. had the stone he was carving and worked at it now and then. 'Well, fire away!' he said.

74

I asked of his first impressions of the *anima* and he said it came in his dream of the white dove when the little girl stood beside him; she was like his eldest daughter. He had this dream at Christmas time in 1913. It was a momentous dream ranking in quality with his early dream at the Rhine Fall at the age of four.[12]

He was sitting in the loggia of an old, beautiful and impressive castle; the loggia was at the top. He sat in a gilded chair. To his left was a table with gilded legs and a top of wonderful green stone, marble of a special kind (*vert du mer*), or emerald – it was the vivid green of an emerald. Around the table were his children. His wife was not there. He sat gazing out through an arched window which had no glass in it; outside was the clear blue sky, not a cloud in sight. Suddenly a white bird like a seagull or a white dove flew in and perched on the table beside him. He signalled to the children not to speak and waited. The bird disappeared; it was no longer there – this puzzled him greatly. Then he was aware of a small girl of about eight years of age standing at his right side; she had fair hair like his eldest daughter. She ran to join the children and afterwards returned for a little. Then she disappeared. Shortly after the white dove reappeared and perched on the table and said, 'I can only come in the early part of the night when the master of the doves is engaged with the twelve dead men.'[13]

At the time he could make nothing of the dream but later he linked the white dove with Hermes – it was the spiritual element. And he recognised the green table as the *Tabula Smaragdina* of Hermes Trismegistos on which the basic elements of alchemical wisdom were engraved. The dream foreshadowed his work on alchemy.

He spoke also of another dream which he had about 1925:

There was fighting between Germans and Italians in North Italy. He was escaping in a carriage drawn by horses; someone was driving this vehicle. They reached the plains of Lombardy and he thought, 'Here we are safe.' They then came to a beautiful ducal palace; it stood in extensive grounds enclosed within a wall. Before them a gate stood open and beyond, in the wall at the opposite side, was another open gate. They drove in intending to pass right through; but at the castle steps the coachman jumped down – he had to stop. Then the gates closed. He knew they were imprisoned, yet had the feeling that he would nevertheless escape.

It was later that he came to see in this dream a reference to alchemy, for he discovered parallels to the castle and the closing of the gates in an old alchemical text, the *Artis Auriferae*. The dream, as he saw it, was a prevision, an anticipation of his research, his captivation by alchemy.[14]

8th January 1957

I asked about the negative aspect of the anima, and he said, 'Well, we become aware of things first when they seem to be against us, to go in an opposite way. That calls our attention to them.'

He mentioned how once, when he was painting, he distinctly heard the voice of a woman saying, *'this is art'*. This happened at a time when his work on a book he was writing had come to a halt – he could not get on with it. The meaning of the incident seemed to be that his writing could be regarded simply as art, as if truth did not matter and that he might write novels or something of the kind equally well. It was the voice of a woman he knew, an artist who had come to work in Zürich and had had a very great influence on a former colleague of his at the Burghölzli – an unfavourable influence. So when he heard her voice saying *'this is art'* he realised that this was, as it were, the voice of the woman who had led his friend astray, and so he could deal with it. This occurred at a very difficult time in 1913, when he was about to resign his post in the university as a lecturer in psychiatry. He could not continue to teach because he had studied Freud's way and also Adler's, and had seen that they both had something which was too narrow. So he had to find his own way, and it was tempting to think, as for a moment he did, of his work as *Art*. But this was a deception, it was the negative aspect of the anima leading him astray.[15]

In the afternoon after lunch I sat in the sun by the lake for an hour and a half. Then tea, and a chat with C.G. and later a walk to the little park.

He was talking about *types*. The extraverted person cannot value anything from the inside, hence the superficiality of much academic psychology – psychological tests for example, or the physical explanations of mental experiences. There is no understanding of the fact that *the mind itself* has its causality; something from the inner life exerts its influence – ideas just arrive in the mind, or symptoms appear. But people assume that these are derived from something outside themselves; the 'cause', however, may lie in their feelings which they have not considered.

He referred to psychological tests and experimental psychiatry, and the vast sums of money spent at Harvard on it – a big building filled with apparatus measuring reactions. One experiment, in which he took part, was to demonstrate an optical illusion of a fast-moving object seeming to go in the opposite direction to that in which he was moving. He asked the professor why they did such things, especially in a 'Department of Human Relations'. What results did they get from the work? He could not answer, but said it was necessary scientific research. C.G. regarded this and similar things as insignificant – they measured so small a part of human reactions it seemed to have no real bearing on psychological understanding.

In the evening C.G. and I were alone for dinner and sat afterwards in the study. He showed me an English Bible of 1540, owned by Thomas Wallis of Tonbridge who, according to the inscription at the beginning, died of 'gout of the stomach' at the age of eighty-five in the year 1775. He showed me also his collection of alchemical works which he said was the best in Switzerland. One volume, he said, was particularly interesting. This was subtitled:

Theatrum Chemicum
Britannicum
containing several Poetical Pieces, of our famous
English Philosophers, who have written
the Hermetique mysterium in their own Ancient Language
Faithfully collected into one Volume with annotations thereon
By Elias Ashmole Esq.
Que est mercuriophilus Anglicus
London
Printed by J. Grifmann for Nath: Brooke at the Angel in Cornhill MDCLII
The Prolegomena by E. Ashmole
26 Jan. 1651 addressed to
All Ingeniously Elaborate Students
In the most Divine Mysteries of Hermetique Learning.

In the main study hang two oil paintings, one on the left of C.G.'s father and the other of his grandfather. He said he had a letter written by his grandfather, who went over the Gottard Pass in a coach with horses and was mighty glad to get to the other side and down to the valley for the road was narrow and difficult.

9th January 1957

Today C.G. received two little booklets entitled *The Divine Law* sent to him by their author, an Indian philosopher named B. Subramanya Iyer, whom he first met twenty years ago at a philosophical congress in Paris. They were inscribed: 'With affectionate regards. 30.11.56.' C.G. recalled that at the Paris conference no one listened to Iyer's lectures because he was speaking like someone of the thirteenth century. It was as if Meister Eckhart was lecturing, and talking of the divine spark in man. People just disregarded him. C.G. cheered him up and invited him to Zürich; but he realised that he was unable to grasp modern thought and could not understand why no one took him seriously. Then when C.G. was in India, he was invited to Mysore State where this man was the guru to the ruler; he was treated very well, stayed in the ruler's guest-house, and was taken for drives in an ancient but comfortable motor car. This incident illustrated C.G.'s open attitude; he saw the interesting side of such a man while realising that he could understand nothing of his own psychology. Also when he was lecturing in Bombay he saw that no one had the slightest idea of what he was talking about, so he began to tell stories of hypnotism and they thought this wonderful!

Later, he referred to the appearance, in analysis, of the archetypes: first comes the *anima*, then the old wise man, and then the *puer aeternus*, for every wise old man must also have the spirit of youth. He mentioned also the archetypes as the representation of the instincts, that is the instincts can be expressed in many ways – there are hundreds of possibilities. But one form is selected because it corresponds to the instinct – it is an image of it.

He spoke of Dorset, which he knew well, and of the White Horse of Cerne Abbas,[16] and other things. Then after dinner Ruth opened *The Listener*, and the first thing she saw was a picture of a White Horse in Yorkshire. C.G. was interested in this picture and mentioned that the ground had been moving and the horse was distorted. All is moving. ... He found Dorset strange and eerie. He had camped somewhere there.

C.G. discussed the point of view of the natural scientist. He said that his own work made no attempt to be philosophical. He was not interested in abstractions; he was concerned only with what he observed, and these things he sought to comprehend. He had a critical mind and could not accept explanations that certain illnesses were caused by certain events. He wanted to study the particular illness, to see what *it* was. Life is not only what we expect it to be. People want to get at *reality*; they seek, for example, to dismiss a delusion merely because it does not conform to 'reality'. But the delusion itself is something; one cannot deny its reality because it is unusual.

He spoke of a dream he had years ago at Bollingen at a time when only the first tower was built. He was alone there for some days, perfectly quiet and at home with nature. He dreamt that he heard music of various instruments, accordions, violins, and so on, and saw a long procession of people walking by the side of the lake, coming from the direction of Schmerikon. When they reached the Tower they divided, one column passed on one side and one on the other. It was so vivid that he woke wondering what they could be doing. He did not realise he had been dreaming and got up and pulled the shutter aside to see these people. There was no one there, nothing but the light of the moon on a clear night.

He went back to bed and fell asleep. The same dream returned, but in it he dreamt that he thought it to be a dream although in fact it was real. Then he woke, and again looked out having pulled the shutter aside.

At the time he could make nothing of this dream. It occurred about thirty years ago, and only last year he came across an account written by an old historian in Lucerne, R. Cysat (1545–1614), who made a collection of the folklore of the area at the beginning of the seventeenth century. Amongst the tales was one of a shepherd on Pilatus. Another man went up and spent a night with him, and in the morning he asked the shepherd about the procession of people playing musical instruments which had passed on either side of the place where they were camped. The shepherd said, 'Oh, you have seen the hosts of Wotan.'

C.G. mentioned this dream as an instance of how the collective unconscious is constellated at certain times, and the great value of this. It is important *to be alone and unhurried* sometimes, for then we are close to nature (as he was on the night of this dream); then we can hear the voice of nature speaking to us.

He told me also how many years ago he and his wife and children were on holiday in a part of Switzerland he knew well. One morning he went on an expedition with the children and returned at lunch time. His wife told him she had been for a walk on the other side of the town where there was a moraine and some small hills. She had seen a very old wooden building at the top of one of these hills and had gone up to look at it. She was very interested in the carving on the door; the wood was dark with age and the carving was of unusually fine quality. C.G. said, 'That's funny! I can't remember such a building and I know that moraine quite well.' He asked her to describe its position again and she suggested that after lunch they should go and see it, it would only take about twenty minutes; it was on the second, or possibly the third, little hill. After lunch they set off and passed the second, third and fourth hill, but no building was there. She was puzzled, but absolutely certain she had seen it. They spent two hours inspecting every hill but could not find it. C.G. said his wife was a particularly well balanced person, full of commonsense: 'She was a sensation type – you couldn't put anything over on her.' But she had that experience; here was a fact, and he could not explain it.

A similar episode occurred much later. C.G. had spoken to Toni Wolff about the Baptistry of the Orthodox in Ravenna where Galla Placidia was buried. Early in the fifth century, after surviving a stormy sea voyage to Ravenna, she had built a church there in fulfilment of a vow. The original church was later destroyed, but her tomb is there.

After visiting the tomb they entered the Baptistry. It was filled with a bluish light, though there was no artificial lighting. C.G. looked round the building and remarked to Toni, 'Isn't it curious? Here are these beautiful mosaics on the west, the east, the south and the north in this octagonal building, and I can't remember seeing them before – it's most remarkable for they are so striking!' In the centre was the font; it was big for it was used for immersion. For twenty minutes they studied the mosaics. C.G. described them as about twice the size of a tapestry hanging in the verandah (which is about six feet by eight feet). Each depicted a baptism scene: one of St. Peter sinking into the sea and our Lord saving him; one of the Israelites in the Red Sea, when the water drowned the Egyptians; one of Naaman the Syrian bathing in the water and being cured of leprosy; and one of our Lord's baptism.

The double symbolism of baptism as a saving of life and as a danger of death was shown in each mosaic. C.G. was particularly impressed by that showing Peter sinking in the sea and stretching out his hand and Jesus reaching for him; this was a most beautiful mosaic of lapis lazuli.

On leaving the Baptistry they went to a shop opposite to get photographs of these mosaics – one of the small shops always found near such places. They were offered pictures of the Baptistry, but none of the mosaics. They went to another shop – no luck – and to several others, but they could not find the photographs they wanted.

Soon after C. A. Meier was going to Italy and C.G. told him to be sure to visit Ravenna and see these mosaics and get pictures of them, or if he couldn't to take photographs. Meanwhile C.G. was giving a seminar in the course of which he mentioned the wonderful mosaics he and Miss Wolff had seen at Ravenna, and he described them in detail.

When Dr. Meier returned from Italy he told C.G. that he had gone to the Baptistry in Ravenna but that there were no mosaics there of the kind he had described. C.G. told this to Toni Wolff who said, 'That's ridiculous, I saw them with my own eyes and you talked of them for about twenty minutes!' 'Nevertheless,' he said, '*there are no such mosaics.*' So at the seminar he said, 'Ladies and gentlemen, I'm sorry but there are no mosaics.'[17]

Here was an experience which two people had, yet how to explain it quite defeated him – he had no suggestion to offer.

He mentioned these things to show how mysterious the mind is, how little we know of it, and how futile it is to 'explain' the manifestations of the psyche away when they do not conform with what we are accustomed to call reality. There are many things in the psyche which we do not understand and have yet to discover, and it was this which initiated his trips to Africa, to the Pueblo Indians, and to India. He wanted to study the mind of the primitive in Africa, people whose point of view was absolutely different from our own. The spectrum of human understanding is infinitely varied and we cannot look on one attitude as right and another wrong in our attempts to explain things beyond our comprehension.

Thus, on the African trip he asked a very intelligent man who was a priest or teacher whether the world was flat, a disc or a globe. 'It's a flat disc,' he replied. 'Well,' said C.G., 'if you see a ship on the horizon, which part do you see first?' 'You see the ship.' 'No,' said C.G., and he referred the question to one of the others who said, 'You see the smoke first, then the masts, and then the ship.' 'That's right,' said C.G., 'and that's because the world is a globe.' 'No,' said the priest, 'that's not true!' 'Well,' said C.G., 'what is the reason?' The priest looked very puzzled; he walked up and down holding his head and for a time could find no answer. Then he said, 'Now I've got it! Allah once made an enormous stone bull and threw it into the ocean but its left horn remained above the surface; that horn is the earth. It sticks up so that you think the earth is a globe, but it could not be a globe for if it were the sea would fall off!' 'Yes,' said the others, 'that is the true reason.'

C.G. was greatly interested for he recognised this as an old Persian idea. These people took it for a fact and were satisfied.

He continued to talk about his visit to Africa, where he first met Ruth Bailey; this was in 1925, and she has remained a close family friend ever since. C.G.'s companions on the journey were Peter Baynes and George Beckwith; Fowler McCormick was to have come but was prevented. On the same boat Ruth was also travelling to Africa with her younger sister whose fiancé they were to meet in Nairobi. She did not meet C.G. on the boat however; he and his companions did not share in the general social activities of the ship but kept apart, reading or talking. They came to be called 'the three Obadiahs' (from the old song, *Obadiah, Obadiah*). In Nairobi everyone stayed in the same hotel, and Ruth's sister was joined by her fiancé. He, of course, showed Ruth every courtesy as well and she became embarrassed when the couple would not allow her to go off on her own and leave them together. In the evening there was a dance in the hotel and Ruth slipped away from her companions into an adjoining lounge; C.G. was sitting there studying maps and she asked if she might, without disturbing him, sit at the same table in order not to appear isolated. He said, 'Oh yes,' and went on looking at his papers. He did not speak for about an hour, and then suddenly said, 'Are you interested in maps?' She said, 'Yes, very.' He then talked of his projected journey and showed her where they were going.

After this meeting Ruth spent some of her time with C.G. and his companions until they left the hotel. They made their way towards Mount Elgon and were encamped in its foothills when C.G. received a letter from the Governor of Uganda asking if he would escort an English lady who was to travel back from Nairobi by way of the Sudan and Egypt – the route he himself planned to follow. Ruth was the person in question, so the meeting in Nairobi paved the way to C.G.'s assent. She made her own way to the site of their camp and was with them for the rest of the expedition – about three months. She had not heard of C.G. previously and knew nothing of his work or reputation. She was well equipped for the eventualities of camp life with a natural ability to meet any situation with humour and good-will, and sound practical sense.[18]

11th January 1957

C.G. referred again to the publication of *The Psychology of the Unconscious* and said he had great difficulty in writing about *sacrifice* – he could not do so for two months. He said he did not write in chapters but continuously, and divided the work later. He felt the book would not be acceptable to Freud because it brought in another principle, namely, that the unconscious acted autonomously. This notion Freud had never admitted into his thinking, and C.G. felt that the publication of the book would mean a break with Freud. His wife reassured him that this would be impossible but he remained unconvinced, and events turned out as he had anticipated.

I referred to the point he had made previously, that his work sprang from his own mind and was not learned from others. As an instance he quoted his interest in trying to understand why Freud and Adler could not agree. Plenty of other people were aware of this but no one saw it as a problem except himself. For him it was a serious matter,

and the study of it led to his work on types. I asked about himself –
how his own attitude fitted in with his classification of types, and he
said he was most definitely the introverted thinking type.

Like Freud, Adler was satisfied with his own theory, for by it he
could explain everything. For him, sex was not the important thing,
but rather that the man wanted to be on top. C.G. saw that there were
these two points of view and each explained a lot, but not everything.
Freud had made his method and his theory one, and this was false.
He would not, and could not, be empirical for you cannot be empirical if you have a fixed theory.

He mentioned that he had a tussle with himself when he realised
that through the word association tests he had found clinical proof of
Freud's theory of repression. The devil said: 'Why not publish it?
It's very interesting and nothing to do with Freud.' But he resisted
this momentary idea and decided there and then to throw in his lot
with Freud. It was a serious decision for it meant sacrificing his academic career and going against the advice of many of his friends. But
he was interested in the truth and 'to hell with an academic career.'

He remarked how important it was for people to be in their own
function – as they really are. For instance how boring it is when
women are always sensible – it is better when they behave a little unexpectedly, irrationally; this makes them more interesting.

Regarding Freudian assumptions that everything was infantile
sexuality which had been repressed, he said, 'Their view is that when
this is realised you must just put it away, forget it and *be cured*. But
you can't put it away without hurt because childish things are very
valuable – the dependence, the interest, the expectant attitude. This
is the *puer aeternus* and you need it, especially in old age for it *keeps
people healthy*. So it is a bad blunder to try to get rid of it; moreover,
you *cannot* just dispose of it.' He said he often asked what *sublimation*
really was and he could never get an answer. It is just a term and has
no reality. You can't change people to fit a theory.

I asked him for his ideas in the treatment of manic-depressive
patients. He thought they were very difficult, but a good plan was to
put them to bed when, as often, they became irritable before either a
manic or a depressed phase.

He cited also two cases of depression. One was a woman who had depressions and a fear of going to Paris. Having remained well for two years, and being eager to see the pictures in the Louvre – she was a highly educated person – she went to Paris with a friend. On the day they arrived there she and her friend were killed by a taxi. The other was the case of a man who was afraid to go up steps into public buildings such, he said, as the steps to the British Museum. This man was in Berlin during the civil troubles before Hitler; there was firing in a street and people ran into houses for shelter. He was outside a public building and rushed up the steps to seek safety, but on the steps 'a bullet found him' and he died.

Apart altogether from psychological discussions, I have noted again and again in general conversation with C.G. how he always gets the facts straight before he makes any comment, and when anything is obscure he questions people until he is sure he understands their meaning. This is very typical of his work and of his attitude, he takes nothing for granted, but wants the facts. He is always ready for something new or unexpected; this is why he has no final theories.

On a walk this evening he asked if I had ever heard a sermon upon the parable of the unjust steward. I said I hadn't. 'No,' he said, 'the theologians never preach about that, for Christ praised the man who had cheated or, in other words, was fully conscious.'[19]

After dinner we sat on the verandah, C.G. behind the little table wearing, as usual, a blue apron, and on the table lay the stone he was carving of the family lineage on the male side. Now and then he chipped at the letters with an expert touch. He mentioned that the inscription was in Latin: 'You see, Latin is the correct, dignified language in which to address the ancestors.'

He added that when he was given an honorary degree at Harvard there was a Latin oration, and he was presented with a 'parchment'. He was particularly interested to see how they had translated the word 'unconscious' into Latin, and it was *mens vacua*, the unknown or unexplored mind. He had been described as the explorer of the unconscious, and he thought this phrase particularly apt.

Later he showed me the knife which long ago had broken into four pieces with a loud report. He had it mounted on a piece of thick paper, and he wrote a description under it. He also spoke of the table which had split with a sudden sharp crack; it was a walnut table which had been part of his grandmother's dowry and it was about seventy years old. Both these events were unexplained.[20] They had happened shortly before he met the mediumistic girl about whom he wrote his dissertation *On the Psychology and Pathology of so-called Occult Phenomena*.[21]

At the same time he showed me a small tumbler of slightly tinted (red or pink) glass, and the rim at the top was sharp all round. He said that at the moment his wife's mother died the upper part of the glass had broken off. And he referred again to the experience in the Baptistry at Ravenna as yet another unexplained event.

A point of interest to me was that he had kept this knife carefully since 1898, and also the glass later. It was interesting, too, that he had not written a note on the paper on which the knife was mounted until this evening.

12th January 1957

At breakfast this morning C.G. spoke of his visit to Paris in 1902. He never saw Charcot,[22] who had retired, but he attended Janet's[23] lectures. He found them terribly boring – no fertilising ideas at all. Janet never knew his patients; he was the opposite of Freud who could never see beyond his patients, but saw them only through his own theory. Janet was typical of French psychology, which was still of the seventeenth and eighteenth centuries when the French were the centre of Europe. The French did not travel; he had read an article in *Le Matin* about this. They looked on foreigners as barbarians, and why go to see them? They had all they needed. The French language was spoken by all polite, educated people; thus in Basle, French was quite *de riguer* amongst the patrician families. Even Leibnitz[24] wrote his works in French.

He mentioned the famous tapestry in the museum in Zürich. It depicts a treaty made with one of the French kings, and shows the French in gorgeous dresses and robes, and the Swiss delegation in top hats and black coats, like a collection of elders –'Nothing outside, it was all inside, and they were very clever, very cunning. It is the best summary of French and Swiss psychology – you get the whole thing. You have to know these things to understand the psychology of French patients.'

86

He was in Paris for months but never got to know a French family. There were plenty of students, but no meeting them outside the lecture rooms. The French would be very polite if you were buying something from them or if they wanted something from you; otherwise all was on the surface. They were like that before the Revolution. Then came Napoleon and *La Grande Armée* – but still on top, and everyone else nowhere. They are like that still, so they make wonderful dresses to sell – all on the surface.

It was totally different when he went to London and lived in a little hotel near the British Museum.

He showed me a letter from an American patient whom he had treated for a schizophrenic breakdown over twenty years ago. She wrote: 'You told me at the time that it, the break, was my *one* big chance, and I thought you were only trying to give me the courage to fight through. But you were right, and I have the proof of it now. However, if I hadn't had the great fortune to get to you, that break would have been my complete ending, and none of the good fortune I listed above would have happened.'

This evening we are sitting again in the study, as has been customary all through this visit – C.G. in his chair, reading or playing patience, Ruth reading on the couch, and myself in a chair by the desk with a shaded lamp, writing notes. Very little conversation.

REFERENCES

1 C. G. Jung, *Wandlungen und Symbole der Libido*, written in 1911 and published the following year. The work was first translated into English by Dr. Beatrice M. Hinkle and was published under the title *Psychology of the Unconscious* by Moffat Yard & Co., New York, in 1916, and by Kegan Paul, London, 1917. In 1956 the translation by R. F. C. Hull of a new and extended edition was published in Jung's Collected Works as Volume 5, *Symbols of Transformation*.

2 C. G. Jung, *The Psychogenesis of Mental Disease*, CW Vol. 3, I, *The Psychology of Dementia Praecox* (first published in 1907).

3 C. G. Jung, *Two Essays on Analytical Psychology*, CW Vol. 7, II, *The Relations between the Ego and the Unconscious* (first published in 1916, and in English translation the following year).

4 C. G. Jung, *Psychological Types*, CW Vol. 6. Jung's work on types was first published in 1921.

   Jung describes the development in his thought at this time in *Memories, Dreams, Reflections*, Chapter VI, 'Confrontation with the Unconscious', pp. 186–88.

   See also Barbara Hannah, *Jung: His Life and Work*, pp. 126–27.

5 Jung's daughter and son-in-law.

6 The dream and Gerard Dorn's text are described in C. G. Jung, *The Archetypes and the Collective Unconscious*, CW Vol. 9, Part I, paras. 334ff.

7 Jung recounts this incident in *Memories, Dreams, Reflections*, Chapter XI, 'On Life After Death', p. 281.

8 Sigmund Freud, *Totem and Taboo: Resemblances between the Psychic Lives of Savages and Neurotics* (1912).

9 *The Secret of the Golden Flower*, translated by Richard Wilhelm, *Commentary* by C. G. Jung, first published in English in 1931. The *Commentary* is also published separately, and in *Alchemical Studies*, CW Vol. 13, I.

10 Marie-Louise von Franz describes the experience in its full context as a synchronistic event in *C. G. Jung: His Myth in Our Time*, Chapter XII, p. 238.

11 Dionysius the Areopagite, author of early alchemical works.

12 C. G. Jung, *Memories, Dreams, Reflections*, Chapter I, 'First Years', pp. 25–26.

13 *Ibid.*, Chapter VI, 'Confrontation with the Unconscious', p. 166.

14 *Ibid.*, Chapter VII, 'The Work', pp. 194–96.
    In *C. G. Jung: His Myth in Our Time*, Chapter X, 'Mercurius', pp. 201–3, Marie-Louise von Franz places the dream in a wider context.

15 In *Memories, Dreams, Reflections*, Jung writes of this experience in Chapter VI, 'Confrontation with the Unconscious', pp. 178–79.

16 In fact the figure at Cerne Abbas is not a horse, but a giant carrying a club. It is an ancient fertility symbol, and in the past childless women would walk up to it in the expectation that this would enable them to conceive.

17 Jung mentioned the mosaics during the *Tantra Yoga Seminar* of 1932. He describes the whole experience in *Memories, Dreams, Reflections*, Chapter IX, 'Travels', *Ravenna and Rome*, pp. 265–66.

18 See Barbara Hannah's description in *Jung: His Life and Work*, pp. 165ff.

19 C. G. Jung, *Psychology and Religion*, CW Vol. 11, VI, *Answer to Job*, para. 696: 'In Christ's sayings there are already indications of ideas which go beyond the traditionally "Christian" morality – for instance the parable of the unjust steward, the moral of which agrees with the Logion of the *Codex Bezae*, and betrays an ethical standard very different from what is expected. Here the moral criterion is *consciousness*, and not law or convention.' (In a footnote he quotes the *Codex Bezae*: 'Man, if indeed thou knowest what thou doest, thou art blessed; but if thou knowest not, thou art cursed, and a transgressor of the law.')

20 C. G. Jung, *Memories, Dreams, Reflections*, Chapter III, 'Student Years', pp. 108–9.

21 Jung used this dissertation as the inaugural address for his medical degree, delivered before the Faculty of Medicine in the University of Zürich in 1902. It is published in *Psychiatric Studies*, CW Vol. I, I.

22 Jean Martin Charcot (1825–93). With his followers, he established what became known as the Salpêtrière School. He influenced the development of neurology in his time, and was renowned for his work on hysteria and the use of hypnotism.

23 Pierre Janet, prominent in the research on the use of hypnotism at Charcot's Clinic at Nancy.

24 Gottfried Wilhelm Leibnitz (1646–1716).

SUMMER 1957

Bollingen, 2nd July 1957

Arrived in Bollingen. Very hot day, and I was tired from the journey. We had dinner by the lake; the plan is to bring the wooden table beside the lake, and everything is carried out by Ruth Bailey and me.

The Tower is an amazing place. The entrance opens into a court-yard which has two exits, both with doors which bar; there is an outer space, also enclosed by a wall and by part of the house, and again a barred gate.

There is only one door into the house, as there is at the house in the Seestrasse, and this door is very heavy with an immensely strong lock and two yale locks. The windows are all small and barred including those upstairs. The hall leads to the kitchen; this is the base of the original tower which C.G. built in 1923. Formerly the kitchen door was the main entrance to the house so it, too, is heavy with a very sturdy lock; the door leading upstairs to the study and the new room (built in 1956–57) can also be locked.

C.G. sleeps in the old tower, so he can be quite isolated. If a robber entered through the front door he could still get no further unless he blew off the locks. So it is like a fortress and quite mediaeval in character.[1]

6th July 1957

At breakfast, speaking of concentration C.G. said he became so con-centrated when he was writing that he did not notice simple inter-ruptions. Yesterday he had been writing in the morning for two hours when Ruth came to say it was time for lunch. He was quite sur-prised, it was as if he had not been there, and as if he had not done any writing; it was all absorbed, all past.

I mentioned Coleridge and the man from Porlock interrupting him when he was writing *Kubla Khan* so that he could not continue.

89

At once C.G. asked, 'What did the man want? What was his message?' I did not know. 'But that was very important', C.G. went on, 'it must have touched a complex – made a hole into the unconscious, and what he was writing disappeared. Also we have to ask why such a person as Coleridge was up in the air with his feet off the ground.' It was remarkable how he got straight to the point – to me a new one – and made the whole picture alive.[2]

Speaking of ideas of God, he said he had had a Kantian training, and spoke of *Ding an Sich*, God like that, not our idea of God, but God as something unknowable. All over the world people have ideas of God, but these are their subjective ideas and not objective.

He said of good and evil that we must always have both, an upper implies a lower; the good implies the not-good as the light the shade. Our subjective point of view was always just that, and we could not make dogmas from it. Things are what they are, a tree is simply a tree; if we say it is a 'good' tree that implies our relationship to it but says nothing about the tree; it may be 'bad' for some other animal.

He has been writing about flying saucers,[3] of which we know nothing; all we know is that *something* has been observed. It might well come from Mars or some other source in space. Two forms are described: one is circular and another cigar shaped; the latter could contain, as tablets in a tube, the former. He mentioned a record in an old newspaper of which a few copies exist in the library in Zürich, and one has a picture exactly like those we see today. Very few pictures exist although there are too many records to be dismissed as nothing.

We say things are 'nonsense' when they do not fit in with our generally accepted ideas. But when people speak of something as 'only imagination' he points to cars or aeroplanes and says that before they were finally constructed they were 'only imagination', for imagination *is* something.

7th July 1957

After breakfast, sitting in the shade where we had the table, I spoke to C.G. about obsessions and their element of secrecy. He agreed, and said that intuitive people were often asked, 'What shall we do now?'– they anticipate the future.

Aug 1

After breakfast — sitting in the shade
where we had the table. I spoke to
C.G. about obsessions + their secret
element. He agreed + said that many
intuitive people ~~this was~~ were always
asked — what shall we do now? — They
are always anticipating the future   The
obsessional always has a skeleton in the
cupboard

I asked about people waking up in
a dream + just before the climax + I
said it was ": they feared something in
themselves — This was an answer to a
question by C.G's son Franz.   . C.G.
said that often it was because something
in their unconscious clashed with their
accepted views + gave an example of a
theologian — a patient of his   who had a
repetitive dream of being on a
mountain + below was a wood +
in the wood a lake which he knew was
there although he hadn't seen it. Then
in a later dream the story was carried
further + the priest was in the wood +
came to the water   there was a 'break'
[?] a slight movement of the water by the breeze'
+ he woke up + frightened. Well,
said C.G. that it a familiar theme +
have you any associations — I asked what

A page from one of the notebooks

Following a remark made by C.G.'s son, Franz Jung, who arrived last night with two of his sons, I raised a question about people waking in a dream just before the climax, and suggested it was because they feared something in themselves. C.G. said that it was often because something in their unconscious clashed with their accepted views. He gave an example of a theologian who had come to him. This man had a repetitive dream of being on a mountain; below was a wood, and in the wood a lake which he knew was there although he had not seen it. In a later dream the image was carried further and the priest was in the wood and came to the lake. There was a 'breath', a slight movement of the water by the breeze, and he woke very frightened. 'Well,' said C.G., 'that is a familiar theme, have you any associations?' I asked what was familiar, and he said it was like the stirring of the waters in the story in the Bible;[4] it meant that the man could be cured, or that a cure was possible, but it would mean giving up his theological views, or altering them, and this he feared to do.

He went on to speak of the natives in Africa – they had a natural psychology. During his visit to Mount Elgon he had noticed how accurately the natives, among whom he spent some time, observed the characteristics of people in his party. He was himself always careful of his emotions, and was reserved and kept something back; so they respected him and regarded him as old and wise. He was fifty but his hair was white, and therefore (as their hair is never white except in very old age) they thought he was about a hundred years old. They would bring him their dreams and ask if they were favourable or not; if the dreams were unfavourable they would not move that day.

I mentioned that the manifestations of hysteria had changed; for example in India and Burma the Indians got the classical hysterical symptoms and the British did not. He said it was the same here, people hardly ever got the old hysterical symptoms nowadays.

C.G. had been reading a paper by a Mr. Routh (Fellow of All Souls) on the possibility of a new Reformation. This article was very good, he said; but it missed the really important point – that a reformation cannot come from historical research or such parallels but only from the heart of individual experience. So it must be today, an event springing from the present time. The teaching of the past, for example of St. Paul or of Jesus, can be edifying, but *in itself* does nothing; Paul himself had a sudden revelation. Unless there is a personal religious experience – realising from the inside what it means – nothing happens. Such an experience can take many forms, for instance falling in love; anything which is really lived.

8th July 1957

Long talk with C.G. I asked him about the dream of the white bird again.[5] He said it had remained a mystery to him for a long time. At first he thought the 'twelve dead men' referred to the twelve days before Christmas for that is the dark time of the year, when traditionally the witches are about. To say 'before Christmas' is to say 'before the sun lives again', for Christmas Day is at the turning point of the year when the sun's birth was celebrated in the Mithraic religion (the great competitor of early Christianity) – the turning point was the night of Christmas Day and Boxing Day. Only much later did he relate the dream to Hermes and the twelve doves.

I also asked again about the table breaking at Basle. This event happened about the time he met the mediumistic girl; and the breaking of the bread knife also occurred about then. The table was round and was the one they had their meals on. This was just a strange experience and not a religious one for the latter would have led to other things. These two experiences remained isolated.[6]

But the meeting and subsequent experiments with the mediumistic girl were important for him because here he got his first glimpse of the fact that there was another world (the unconscious) which had a life of its own quite apart from the life of consciousness. The girl, in her trances, was living ahead of her actual age of fifteen-and-a-half, and from this he concluded (later) that the unconscious was timeless – all her life was there already. The girl was clever and afterwards became the leading dressmaker in Basle and made most beautiful dresses. She died when she was twenty-six, of tuberculosis.

I asked about his functional types[7] and those of Freud – anal erotic and so on. He said the latter were quite uninteresting and were the result of Freud's captivation by the anima, for only women, because of childbirth and children, were interested in such things. But his functional types were described because they were true in general, and were understood in general. Everyone knows what is meant by thinking and feeling, they lead somewhere.

He said it had been very difficult for him just before the First War, after his break with Freud. In July 1914 he was asked to go to Aberdeen to lecture on schizophrenia[8] and he had been, at this time, most distressed by disturbing visions, and then by a dream which recurred three times over a period of several months; the details varied, but the central theme depicted the polar region of ice sweeping over and swamping Europe and civilization. At first he took the dream personally, not knowing what else it could signify. But when war broke out his fears that some personal disaster might befall him were relieved for he realised with certainty that the dreams referred to the catastrophe of the war.[9] From Aberdeen he returned hom through Germany, sometimes in troop trains. At Cologne, or near there, he saw a Zeppelin shot down and the pilot hanging caught in a tree.

Talking later of his writing he said that when he published his work on alchemy[10] people said it was nonsense. A professor in Oxford wrote saying that he had read the book and found it most interesting, but no proof was given. 'But,' said C.G., 'the book is full of proofs! What could he have wanted as a proof? Something he could explain "scientifically", or take a photograph of?' What C.G. regarded as important was that people thought as the alchemists had done – they had certain experiences, and still have. He is interested in the *experience*, not in 'proving'.

11th July 1957

Freud assumed the censor; but as it was an unconscious factor, which is a form of dissociation, we could never know it. So he inferred that every sharp object appearing in a dream was a penis and all hollow objects represented the vagina. 'But,' C.G. asked him, 'what if you dream of a penis?' 'Oh, then,' said Freud, 'the censor hasn't worked.' This, of course, is a *petitio principii*.

I asked about Eugen Bleuler and his attitude towards dreams. C.G. said he never took them seriously; he might ask C.G. what he thought a certain dream meant, but his reply to the explanations or suggestions put forward was always, 'That's all nonsense!'

C.G. said that Bleuler later published a history of the Burghölzli

Hospital and mentioned almost everyone who had ever worked there, but he made no reference to Jung. Yet it was he (C.G.) who had made the Burghölzli famous through his work on word association tests and his published work. Someone wrote to Bleuler and asked why he had not mentioned Jung in his book and he replied, 'Oh, he's famous already – everyone has heard of him!' But why leave him out?

We talked of evil and he mentioned the odd principle in the New Testament: 'To him that hath shall be given, and from him that hath not shall be taken away what he hath.'[11] (I mentioned that one English version gave the translation 'taken away what he *seemeth* to have', but he said this was not so in the German translation). He said it was unjust as a principle. Also he mentioned Christ as false to his teaching in riding into Jerusalem on an ass – a man walking is nothing – it was a recognition of the earthly saviour coming in triumph. Following this he cursed the barren fig tree, but it was not the season of figs. It was like a man kicking the stone he has stumbled on; that is, he was suggesting that Christ had made a mistake in riding on the ass and that his cursing of the fig tree was a show of temper which often accompanies such a slip – as it is with us always.

In Genesis reference was made to the Lord saying that everything he had created was good, but how could we know this for man was not made until the last day of creation?

C.G. often makes amusing and penetrating remarks. For instance in St. Gallen he asked a man the way, and the man told us as well that we ought to go and see the Rhine (or a tributary of it) in flood a little way off and added other information. C.G. remarked afterwards drily, 'These extraverts are quite useful!'

He enjoys the countryside all the time as we drive in Fowler McCormick's car, and comments on the geological formations. We drove from St. Gallen to Rorschach on Lake Constance today, then we turned south along the Rhine which flows into the lake. We went on to Sargans – famous for its wine and its fortifications – and then along a magnificent road by the Walensee to Weesen. Here we had anticipated having a wonderful dinner although in fact it turned out to be quite ordinary.

13th July 1957

Today C.G. read a short story published by a patient who had consulted me; he regarded it as sinister and commented on the patho-
logical features. It reminded him of a young woman he had once seen
who had the idea she was living on the moon (the moon is the female
principle). He treated her and got her over it. But it was very tricky,
and he felt it was of paramount importance to make contact with her.
Her story conveyed the essence of her problem and he accepted it un-
critically. After three weeks, and many hours with him going over
these ideas, she handed him a 'pocket', a little bag, very heavy; in it
was a small loaded revolver. 'What is this?' he asked. She said she
had carried it for the three weeks, and if he had failed her or refused
to believe her she would have shot him. All the time, but without
knowing why, he had feared she might do something to harm him,
but he had not dared to speak of this to her.

Later she married and had a family, and as an old woman she wrote
to him saying that after all the years she still could hardly believe that
she had once been insane and in the clinic.

He spoke of the difficulty people have in thinking of the psyche as
anything but a personal, subjective possession. Yet ever since his experience with the mediumistic girl he had regarded the psyche as an
objective phenomenon with its own autonomous laws.

C.G. was in wonderful form today and most amusing, reading out
bits from an American magazine – one about a thinking horse, and
another of a dog behaving peculiarly, and its owners called in a *dog
psychiatrist*! – this amused him tremendously. All the same it could
have happened that the owner of the horse was able to influence it,
transmit some impulse to it, so that it would count by tapping its
foot.[12]

He went on to mention various spiritualistic phenomena in which
objects became materialised. He quoted an instance when an ac-
quaintance of his took part in such an experiment. A hand materialised and his friend grasped it; it had no bones, and gradually, while
his friend held it, it dissolved away. These queer things do happen,
he remarked. On another occasion a head appeared; his friend put a
glass tube into its mouth, and connected this by a rubber tube to a
solution of calcium oxide; the carbon dioxide in the breath from this

head passing into the solution through the tube precipitated a deposit of calcium carbonate on the vessel.

In the evening we had a particularly nice dinner by the lake, and a bottle of 1945 Château Neuf du Pape. Ruth described it as a pre-celebration of his birthday, and I had just given him some cigars as a birthday present.

14th July 1957

C.G. told me that years ago when there was only the one tower built, he came in the winter and lived here alone for two weeks. It was absolutely quiet with no one about and no sounds except the wind and the waves. Hans came to help with some domestic jobs and then went home. It was then that he had the remarkable dream of the hosts of Wotan coming from the direction of Schmerikon.[13] These things occur, he said, when you are alone and exposed to your thoughts and to the unconscious. Many people cannot bear to be alone for any length of time but it is valuable.

At this same period, and when they were preparing a meal (C.G. and Hans) he distinctly heard someone call his name –'Dr. Jung'. He went to the door but no one was there. He asked Hans if he had heard anything and he said, 'No.' Shortly after both he and Hans heard his name called and both ran to the door but there was no one there. Hans was astonished and said he had heard a voice with his own ears. Yet there was no explanation.

After tea C.G. read a poltergeist story from a magazine. He said there were many attested stories of the kind. One he mentioned, from Australia, was of a youth (it is always an adolescent) on whom, or around whom, stones fell. He was put in a tent with people inside it with him and ten men watching outside. Stones fell from the inside of the canvas tent and nothing was observed outside. The boy went to another place because he was very distressed; then he went to his grandfather to get his help in overcoming the tendency to cause the stones to fall.

C.G. said these poltergeist phenomena happened in adolescence and often appeared as a sort of dissociation, as in the case of the mediumistic girl. Often boys and girls between fourteen and sixteen or so did the most crazy and dangerous things, and played all sorts of silly tricks. He had done so himself. This might be linked to the same tendency, a sort of possibility of development. I asked about Oliver Lodge's experiences.[14] Of course he knew all about Raymond – it's amazing how extensive his knowledge is, and the scope of his memory. He said it all seemed very silly; it had some sort of truth in it, but Oliver Lodge never considered it from the psychological angle.

C.G. mentioned that he had a dream of his sister six weeks after she died. He was in some kind of castle and went to meet her at the station. He met her, and she was about a head taller than himself. He walked beside her and glanced at her. She then made herself the same height as he was. In life she had been shorter than C.G.

He added no comment or explanation of this dream. But he went on to mention three dreams he has had of his father. His father died in 1896. He was a highly educated man, a scholar knowing six or seven oriental languages, Hebrew, Arabic, Ethiopian, and others. But he let these things slip from him and lost himself in chatting and talking to people. In the first dream his father was taller than C.G. In life he was shorter. C.G. saw him in his house, and there was a mediaeval library as big as the Reading Room at the British Museum. This meant the development of the intellectual side.

C.G. dreamt again about his father in 1922 – that is twenty-six years later in October or November. In the dream his father appeared in C.G.'s house in Küsnacht; he was much smaller than in life. C.G. thought he would tell him of the events which had happened since his death in 1896 and show him his wife and family; but it seemed that his father had come for a consultation and he asked C.G. about problems of married life. (His marriage to C.G.'s mother had not been altogether a success). So C.G. gave him a sort of lecture on marriage and its problems. The following spring C.G.'s mother died. It was as though his father had anticipated her death and meeting her again and wanted to prepare for the event.

In the third dream his father was taller – he had increased in stature and was taller than C.G. They were in an ancient Indian town not far from Agra, or Chataputri, and C.G. was an adolescent. Two young workmen in a shed opposite were behaving in a way like poltergeists and making a fearful row by throwing bits of timber about in a purposeless manner. This dream was in 1950 – twenty-eight years later, just when C.G. was writing, or preparing to write, *Aion*.[15] In the dream C.G. was a youngster. It was a sort of initiation, just as in poltergeist stories of adolescents there is an element of initiation. Thus the mediumistic girl could behave, in her trance, like a woman of thirty.

Bollingen

This is really C.G. in stone, the expression of himself, quite apart from the world.

The first part to be built was the round tower on the left; there is a large kitchen and upstairs three rooms.

There is no electric light in the Tower, only oil lamps, and the cooking is done in the open hearth and on an oil stove. The water supply is from a pump in the hall, and below it is a big stone basin. There are many stone carvings. In the wall of the loggia are two very small apertures; through one it is possible to see the path leading to the house, and through the other the path to the front door.

Breakfast is at about 8.30 and we have it outside in the shade or, if it is raining, in the kitchen. After breakfast we may sit and read or talk. Washing up is done by Ruth and Hans (or by Ruth and me); C.G. takes no part in this activity. He has finished writing on flying saucers and now has to write a short paper on conscience, a subject he finds of very limited interest; but, he says, people are interested and give it too much significance. I mentioned the Roman Catholic bishop in Ireland who preached that people must not go by their conscience but by what the Church said. This, he said, makes people feel safe and they need not think.

In the evening after dinner we may sit outside or in the loggia in the courtyard, reading by the light of a paraffin lamp. C.G. reads the newspapers very fully. When it rains we sit in the little room at the base of the second tower. The big fireplace is at the back occupying nearly the whole width of the wall, and round the side of the rest of the room is a stone seat covered with tiling, and on this some cushions. The space is small; on two evenings we (C.G., Ruth and I) sat there with our chairs absolutely jammed together reading by the light of an old lamp suspended from the ceiling. This evening we are doing the same. What an odd setting! If only those who read his books could see C.G. here, in his shirt sleeves and an old pullover, and socks (with a hole in them!). Here much of the cooking is done. This evening, for example, C.G. cooked an excellent dinner, crouching on one of the small chairs (which are made in the Tessin). He is very particular indeed about every detail of the cooking. We had pork chops, and he made the sauce for these with flour and water and a glassful of wine. Then he made the salad at the table, cutting up tiny bits of garlic and mixing these on the wooden spoon with some salt and pepper (I think). Then we had some crushed plums (a purée) which came from the garden in Küsnacht, and some kirsch. Very good it was. Then into this room at the base of the tower where we now sit.

The second tower begins at the first storey and this room is really part of the extension built as the second stage of the whole structure. Following it came the upper part of the tower; then the containing wall, then the loggia in the courtyard and then the top storey in 1957, the final bit.

15th July 1957

This afternoon, following a rest C.G. spent about an hour and a half cutting up wood for the fire. This driftwood was collected by Hans (and by me) from the lake. He is surprisingly agile and gives very strong strokes with the bill hook. Then he and I packed the wood *à la Suisse*. Afterwards we had dinner in the loggia in the courtyard where C.G. lit the fire. Just now Ruth is busy in the house and C.G. and I are sitting in the loggia – he reading his newspapers as he does every evening, and I write this, smoking one of the cigars I gave him as a birthday present. This afternoon Ruth and Hans, with the boat, spent a long time removing the weeds and reeds which had been driven down the lake and were lying in front of the Tower.

Each day Ruth feeds the coots with bread – nice little birds – father, mother and two youngsters; and sometimes, not always, the swan family appears – three cygnets and one or other, or both, parents.

Another day Hans and I spent about two hours hauling blocks of compressed coal, by pulley, up to the loft at the top of the newest addition to the building.

Later, talking with C.G., I asked him if his early experiences with his parents had influenced his interest in psychological things. He said he thought not; his father's religious teaching was unclear, and while in one way he believed it as a child it was always very unreal. His mother never discussed religious things and avoided his questions and put them aside. He went on to say that in his early years he had learnt nothing from his teachers which had any bearing on the development of his own thought. This had always come from within his own mind. His father taught him Latin from the age of six and for this he was always grateful.

He said that after his break with Freud he felt with great insistence the need for some meaning in life. He could see that in past ages people had lived by a myth, that is they had some central idea which gave their lives meaning. But, he asked himself, by what myth, what central idea, did he live? He had none. When in the past he had asked his father about Christianity his father could not answer his questions; he had only said, 'Oh, you think too much! You must believe!' 'But,' C.G. replied, 'that's how I'm made, how can I stop thinking? How can I just believe?' But he never got an answer. In this period following the break with Freud the question became a real difficulty for him, and for three years he wrote nothing and did no scientific work but tried (successfully) to come to grips with his own psychology and his beliefs.

He could not understand what people meant when they talked of a personal saviour. How could God have allowed his Son to be crucified? Any father would have fought against such a thing, yet God had exacted it as a sort of requirement from his Son. Various allusions in the New Testament gave him some hint of a continuity between the Old and New Testaments; one was the story of the unjust steward and another the fact that Jesus cursed the barren fig tree. But he could not conceive of any sort of *personal* contact with the figure of Jesus whom he had been told to love as a child and who had died for our sins. Why should his dying be so important? Why was it necessary to placate God in such a way?

I asked C.G. what myth he had found – what central idea, for him, gave meaning to life? At once he replied, 'Oh, that is the collective unconscious.'

Talking of Freud at breakfast he said it was nonsense to write, as Ernest Jones had done,[16] that Freud had conducted a personal analysis on himself. Such a thing was impossible, for any attempt at self-analysis could only be subjective; by no means could he ever get beyond himself, outside himself. It was absolutely necessary in analysis to have another point of view, that of another person.

Freud's myth was that of the primal father so he was inclined to suspect people, and he suspected C.G. and thought he wished to supplant him. But C.G. said he had made his first contact with Freud through contributing clinical proof of his theory of repression, and this had meant that he himself gave up his expectations of an academic career. Two professors wrote telling him it would be professional ruin to throw in his lot with Freud. But C.G. was impelled by a desire for the truth – to find out what was really in the mind. As time went on he learned that Freud would only go a certain way and that he always excluded any idea which did not fit his theory.

When they visited New York together in 1909 they had done some mutual dream-analysis. At one point Freud declined to give his associations on certain dreams; he hesitated and then said, 'No – I cannot risk my authority.' And in that moment, naturally, he lost it.[17] But C.G.'s question gave him a shock and did something to alter his attitude. Freud had once said to him that he should pay no attention to patients, they did not matter. 'What a strange remark, it's from our patients we learn!' C.G. had replied. He went on to tell me that in fact Freud had good feeling and cured his patients by being kind to them.

REFERENCES

1   The road along the northern side of the upper part of the Zürich Lake, passing through Bollingen, was part of the route followed by criminals and adventurers travelling from the east to join the Foreign Legion in Marseilles. Hence the necessity for attention to security.

2   The incident is described in *The Poetical Works of Samuel Taylor Coleridge*, edited by William Michael Rossetti: 'In the summer of the year 1797, the Author, then in ill health, had retired to a lonely farm house between Porlock and Linton, on the Exmoor confines of Somerset and Devonshire. In consequence of a slight indisposition an anodyne had been prescribed, from the effect of which he fell asleep in his Chair at the moment he was reading the following

sentence ... in *Purchas's Pilgrimage*: "Here the Khan Kubla commanded a palace to be built, and a stately garden thereunto: and thus ten miles of fertile ground was enclosed with a wall." The author continued for about three hours in a profound sleep, at least of the external senses, during which time he has the most vivid confidence that he could not have composed less than from two to three hundred lines: if that indeed can be called a composition in which all the images rose up before him as things, with a parallel production of the correspondent expressions, without any sensation or consciousness of effort. On awaking he appeared to himself to have a distinct recollection of the whole, and taking his pen, ink, and paper, instantly and eagerly wrote down the lines that are here preserved. At this moment he was unfortunately called out by a person on business from Porlock, and detained by him above an hour, and on his return to his room, found, to his no small surprise and mortification, that though he still retained some vague and dim recollection of the general purport of the vision, yet, with the exception of some eight or ten scattered lines and images, all the rest had passed away like the images on the surface of a stream into which a stone had been cast. ... Yet, from the still surviving recollections in his mind the Author has frequently purposed to finish for himself what had been originally, as it were, given to him ... but the tomorrow is yet to come. 1816.'

3   C. G. Jung, *Flying Saucers, A Modern Myth of Things Seen in the Skies*, published in English in 1959. See also *Civilization in Transition*, CW Vol. 10, Section V.

4   The pool of Bethesda at Jerusalem where sick people gathered to await the stirring of the water; whoever first stepped into the pool when the waters moved was cured of his disease.

5   The dream related in conversation on 7 January 1957.

6   These incidents are mentioned in the conversation of 11 January 1957.

7   C. G. Jung, *Psychological Types*, CW Vol. 6. The *Functions* are described in Chapter X.

8   C. G. Jung, 'On the Importance of the Unconscious in Psychopathology', published in *The Psychogenesis of Mental Disease*, CW Vol. 3, III. It was first published in the *British Medical Journal* (1914).

9   C. G. Jung, *Memories, Dreams, Reflections*, Chapter VI, 'Confrontation with the Unconscious', pp. 169–70.

10   C. G. Jung, *Psychology and Alchemy*, CW Vol. 12.

11   The final sentence of the parable of the talents. (St. Matthew's Gospel, 25:29).

12   The stories of the mind-reading horse, Lady Wonder, and the canine psychiatrist were read from *Fate* magazine of August 1957 (Clark Publishing Company, Illinois).

13   This experience is mentioned in the conversation of 10 January 1957; Jung describes it in *Memories, Dreams, Reflections*, Chapter VIII, 'The Tower', pp. 217–18.

14   Sir Oliver Lodge, English physicist, born 1851. His original work included investigations on lightning, and on various phenomena of electrolysis, electromagnetic waves, and wireless telegraphy. He was knighted in 1902. From 1901 to 1904 he was President of the Society for Psychical Research. His young son,

Raymond, was killed during the First War, and he communicated with him afterwards through spiritualistic sessions and published these experiences. At a time when many people were bereaved the book made a marked impact. See Sir Oliver Lodge, *Raymond* (revised), London 1922; and *The Survival of Man. A study in unrecognised human faculty* (10th edition), London 1926.

15 C. G. Jung, *Aion*, CW Vol. 9, Part II.

16 Ernest Jones, *Sigmund Freud: Life and Work* (Hogarth Press 1957), Vol. I, Chapter XIV, 'Self-Analysis'.

17 E. A. Bennet, *C. G. Jung*; this incident is described in wider context in the Chapter 'Jung and Freud: Hail and Farewell', pp. 39–40.

SPRING 1959

Küsnacht, 20th March 1959

Arrived at the Haupbahnhof at 2.20 p.m. and was met by Ruth Bailey and Müller [Jung's chauffeur] and so to Küsnacht. Tea on the verandah. C.G. is in good form and looking very fit. He was interested at seeing the dredger arriving, apparently to dredge by the Strandbad.

After tea he went to see a patient and I visited Barbara Hannah. Back at the Seestrasse C.G., Ruth and I strolled in the garden before dinner and had a look at two magnolia trees, one of which was planted last year. Then we went on through the garden to the lake. I asked about a cross which is nailed to the summer house and he said it was from a churchyard (I wonder where).

We had a pleasant chat at dinner. C.G. was glad he had finished work for the term and had only one or two people to see. I reminded him of the man we had met in St. Gallen who told us of the river in flood and his (C.G.'s) remark, 'These extraverts are quite useful!', and he laughed heartily.

Later we went upstairs to the study. He arranged –'as usual' he said – the chair for me under the lamp by his writing table, and he sat by the window reading the evening paper and smoking a cigar; he gave me one. On his writing table is an object I have seen before, sent to him by the Indian Psychiatric Society; it is a carved wooden lotus which opens. They also sent him, years ago, a *dhoti* of cotton which he once put on with much difficulty and amusement. There is also a metal statue of Buddha on the table.

Another feature in the main study is the large Swiss stove of green tiles; this one is quite an architectural feature as it is fitted at an angle. These stoves are easily lit and use little fuel, usually wood. Behind where I sit are the books on alchemy – a remarkable collection.

When C.G. had finished with the newspaper he played patience on a board on his knee, sitting with his feet up on another chair. We sit quite silently, a very peaceful scene. He likes to be quiet in the evenings and let his mind unbend, uncoil.

21st March 1959

After breakfast C.G. and I sat in the garden in the sun and he read my Introduction and part of Chapter 2.[1] He made a few comments as he read. His father was Lutheran, but of the Basle Reformed Church. There were variations between Geneva (Calvin) and Zürich (Zwingli) – the latter was very rational; wooden vessels were used at communion and there were no ornaments, whereas at Basle they were more ritualistic, or more old fashioned.

Coming to my notes about his childhood dream of the underground chamber he said what a tremendous impression it had made upon him.[2] A red carpet led to the dais, just a strip, and on it was a large golden throne. He said that the object which stood upon it, which he took to be a tree trunk, was about four times his height – twelve or fifteen feet – and he corrected my manuscript in pencil accordingly. It had an eye like a demonic god, and his terror at this apparition intensified when his mother's voice called from outside, 'Just look at him, he's the man-eater!'

He told me that he had been writing an autobiography of the first twenty-five years of his life but he was hesitant to publish it because it could so easily be misunderstood, and this could disturb many people who depended upon him. He said it was only two years ago, while he was working on this autobiography, that he suddenly linked the three early episodes of his dream of the cave, the priest and funerals.[3] He often saw funerals for the churchyard was near their house; only at these services did the men appear with polished shoes, black clothes and tall hats. In his mind he linked the dream of the cave with a tomb – like Jesus in the tomb – and with the priest; he thought the priest was a woman. Throughout the years these experiences had been 'islands of consciousness' and now he saw the connection between them for the first time.

As a small child he was taught to pray that Jesus would look after, keep safe, this chicken (himself) and put his wings over him. There was some link between the idea of a chicken and a little cake, and God would not eat the cake. But the devil would eat any amount of cakes like this.[4] All these reflections of his were *a secret* for he thought his parents would not know these things nor understand them; so this separated them from him. He associated his mother's words in the dream of the cave –'That is the man-eater'– with the priest, and it was absolutely terrifying. Then, much later, in the dream in Basle he saw that he must accept the strange idea of God treating the Church with disrespect.[5]

What would a scientist think of such ideas? For him they were impressive and a source of development.

In the afternoon we drove to Bollingen, C.G., Ruth and I. It took half an hour. The Tower looked its best in the warm sunshine and we walked around. C.G. took me to see his carving of Attis at the end of the path near the boat house. The carving, in stone, was a small pillar and had on it Tō ATTEI – to Attis. It was set in the midst of anemones, small wild ones, and C.G. said this was the flower of Attis. He spoke of the story of Attis as one of the most beautiful in antiquity and classed it with that of Apollo and Demeter. On the wall of the Tower he had made a new carving of a woman kneeling; he said she was the mother of Attis.

While we were there C.G. spent much of the time sitting beside a little stream which comes from two springs and runs down to the lake. He had a tool which he said was used by shepherds – a small spade, part of which stood up to make a crook; he had it fixed to a polo stick with a thong at the end. The stick was long and he sat by the stream and cleared the channel with the spade so that the water flowed freely. I asked why he did this and he said he found it was relaxing and let his mind work; he liked to be beside the flowing water which suggested the flow of life and ideas. Ruth said he often did this when, as now, the water in the lake is low. After the snows melt the lake rises and the little streams are usually covered. When he is reflecting in this way C.G. likes to be silent and alone. He never finds it irksome to be alone.

22nd March 1959
We went for a drive to see the grounds which are being prepared for the coming exhibition; it will be held on either side of the lake and connected by a cable railway which is now being constructed. C.G.

wanted to see this and we walked round. He is very interested in such a thing; also in old buildings and houses.

From the site of the exhibition we drove down the Sihl Valley and had coffee with Müller joining us. Then we returned over the Albis Pass. C.G. took great pleasure in the natural surroundings, the trees, the little lake Türler, and in the various views of Zürich. When we got back we walked round the garden and he looked at every plant and flower.

I asked whether he had met James Joyce, and he had done so. He remarked that his writing in *Ulysses* was brilliant at times; he mentioned particularly the detailed description of a piece of paper floating down the river to the sea which he had quoted in his paper on *Ulysses*.[6]

After tea C.G. and I sat in the front garden just behind the wall. I asked some questions about the origin and development of his theory of types. Later he talked of *kinship libido*, the natural bond between people, the link they need to prevent isolation, to be aware of belonging with others of like interest and awareness.

23rd March 1959

C.G. told me to read *Dr. Zhivago*, a novel by the Russian, Pasternak; it was a wonderful picture of the anima. 'You don't know who she is, she's not quite real, too good to be true; and there's something wrong somewhere.' In the library in the evening he said to Ruth, 'If you want to know what the anima is you must read that book!' In *Dr. Zhivago* the anima is absolutely typical, and he (Pasternak) did not know what she was.

Before dinner C.G., Ruth and I went for a walk to the little park by the Strandbad pier. He had just seen a French professor who was very concerned about the real truth of the life of Jesus of Nazareth, the historical Jesus; this man knew all the various versions and was in doubt about the truth. C.G. told him, and repeated to us, an experience he and members of the British Association had when he was in India. They were near Darjeeling, and went up Signal Hill, a well-known place, to watch the sunset. They had the good fortune to get an absolutely clear view of Kanchenjunga which is rare, for the high mountain is usually in cloud. On Signal Hill is a mound of stones;

they are reddish in colour being painted with red oxide of lead, and the Mohammedans pour *ghee* over them. The red represents blood. There are also many very tall bamboos –'as high as the electric standards,' he said, pointing to one in the road. These trees were hung all over with little flags printed with a horse (a special horse which he described but I could not get the details) for this had been a sacred place for many many centuries, since long before Mohammed.[7] It was a marvellous spectacle with the valley in shadow and then the bluish-purple, and out of it all the brilliant fiery setting of the sun. Everyone gazed spellbound at this striking scene, and one of the members of the British Association muttered 'Phew!'– an involuntary exclamation of awe. C.G. said to him, 'What is that you do? You are uttering quite spontaneously the exclamation of awe which has been uttered for countless centuries, and you don't know it!' There was quite a crowd there and Barker, the professor of English from Cambridge, said, 'Now Jung, you must know the famous passage in *Faust* about the setting sun!' And Jung did know it, and recited it.[8] It was a most impressive and highly unscientific spectacle, he said. He repeated the passage from Goethe to us as we sat in the little shed by the pier where, as often before, we had sat after a similar stroll. 'But,' C.G. went on to tell us, 'here was a living myth, for the mountain lit by the sun is said to be the wife of Vishnu; and the myth gives the story and the experience meaning. That is what myths are.'

He spoke of the stupidity of an Anglican parson who had visited him and talked of 'trying to get Truth', as if he could get it in a form he would be able to understand and that it would not be truth otherwise.

In the evening when we were sitting in the library he asked Ruth to show me the pictures in an Italian paper of flying saucers. He had got this paper from an Italian who had taken a photograph of a flying saucer in 1952; he had been thrown out of his photographic club because it was assumed to be a false picture, but recently it has been accepted. C.G. knows a lady in southern Switzerland who is the secretary of an organization which records observations of UFOs, and she sends him reports about them. One was a photograph, which he showed me, of a typical UFO; he had written on the back that it had been taken by an eighteen-year-old girl, the daughter of a parson in California. She had, so he wrote, put her camera in the fork of a tree for a time exposure, and later came to terminate it. When the negative was developed there was the flying saucer. Apparently she had not seen it.

24th March 1959

In the morning we drove to a high point above Küsnacht and sat in the sun and had coffee.

On our return C.G. and I sat in the front garden. I asked about Ernest Jones's remark that on an early visit to Freud he (C.G.) had demonstrated poltergeist phenomena.[9] He said this was utter nonsense; he knew the statement had been made by Freud. The basis of it was this: at the close of their first talk, which lasted thirteen hours, he felt disappointed because the discussion had been restricted by Freud's insistence on explaining everything only in terms of sexuality. C.G. had been thrilled to meet and talk with him and at the end of the conversation he was still full of unresolved expectations. Suddenly there was a loud cracking in the bookcase above Freud's head, a formidable crash as if the wood were expanding and the whole thing coming down. Freud looked up startled, and C.G. said, 'What do you make of that?' He knew at once that it was an extra-corporeal expression of a psychic situation and that it would happen again, though he did not know why. But he told Freud, 'It will happen again,' and at once it did. Freud was aghast though he would not say so; he tried to dismiss it as nothing. But it was a real crash and C.G. told him at the time that it was significant. They examined the bookcase and there was nothing to see. C.G. had had experience of similar incidents – extra-corporeal effects, he called them – and added that these parapsychological things are *exteriorised affects* and happen like complexes – that is they are projected. The crash affected Freud very much but he never sought to explain it. 'If I had never asked Why? in the word association tests,' said C.G., 'I would never have discovered the complexes. But Freud brushed these things aside. There is now an Institute for Parapsychology at Freibourg and the Director comes to consult me.' A similar incident had happened with Eugen Bleuler and when C.G. mentioned parapsychological phenomena to him he said it was all nonsense; but twenty years later he became a spiritualist and had many experiences of this kind. C.G. described the crash in the bookcase as a *synchronistic event*, as acausal. It could not be explained; but it happened, of that there was no doubt. It gave him an odd feeling: 'Now look out! – there might be a split between us.'

We went on to talk of dreams and I mentioned my idea of making dreams and clinical material central in what I would write; he thought this quite a good plan. Speaking of dreams he said we must always ask 'Whose dream?' It was always an individual matter, we cannot generalise; we develop guidelines but not laws. For Freud *all* dreams were wish fulfilments, and he looked on the dream as a means of preserving sleep. C.G. thought that more often than not they failed to keep us asleep.

He talked for a while about Laufe, his early home above the Rhine Fall. Then at tea-time Mrs. Niehus came. She asked about my book. I told her C.G. had mentioned that he had already written much of his autobiography (I remember him talking of the difficulties of writing about his life a year or two ago and perhaps this put the idea into his mind). She said Mrs. Jaffé wanted to publish what he had written. I gave her my Introduction to read. She said my approach was quite different from Mrs. Jaffé's and pressed me to continue. She said mine was more masculine, and the fact that another biography was in preparation should not prevent me from going on with it. C.G. had read it earlier and he also thought it good and on the right lines.

REFERENCES

1 E. A. Bennet, *C. G. Jung* (1961).

2 *Ibid.*, p. 10.
    C. G. Jung, *Memories, Dreams, Reflections*, Chapter I, 'First Years', p. 26.

3 C. G. Jung, *Memories, Dreams, Reflections*, p. 25ff.

4 *Ibid.*, p. 24:
    'Spread out thy wings, Lord Jesus mild,
    And take to thee thy chick, thy child,
        "If Satan would devour it,
        No harm shall overpower it,"
        So let the angels sing!'
    The link between a chicken and a little cake lies in the German word *Küchlein* which means both *chicken* and *little cake*.

5 *Ibid.*, Chapter II, 'School Years', p. 47.

6 C. G. Jung, *The Spirit in Man, Art and Literature*, CW Vol. 15, V, '*Ulysses': A Monologue*, para. 186, Jung quotes: 'Elijah, skiff, light crumpled throwaway, sailed eastward by flanks of ships and trawlers, amid an archipelago of corks, beyond new Wapping street past Benson's ferry, and by the threemasted schooner *Rosevean* from Bridgwater with bricks.'

7 The horse was brought into India in very early times by Aryan invaders, and the horse on the flags hung on the trees in this place of ancient sacred tradition would almost certainly be linked with the fact that it was a sacrificial animal. In the teaching of the Upanishads the sacrifice of the horse had cosmic significance; through it a new state, beyond the human one, was attained. See C. G. Jung, *Symbols of Transformation*, CW Vol. 5, Part Two, VIII 'The Sacrifice', paras. 657, 658.

8 Goethe, *Faust, Part I.* Scene: 'Outside the City Gate' (translated by Philip Wayne).

> *Faust:* 'Ah, happy he who still can hope to rise,
> Emerging from this sea of fear and doubt!
> What no man knows, alone could make us wise;
> And what we know, we well could do without.
> But let not mortal troubles cast their shades,
> Before this hour of sweet content has run,
> Mark, now, the glimmering in the leafy glades,
> Of dwellings gilded by the setting sun.
> Now slants the fiery god towards the west,
> Hasting away, but seeking in his round
> New life afar: I long to join his quest,
> On tireless wings uplifted from the ground.
> Then should I see, in deathless evening-light,
> The world in cradled stillness at my feet,
> Each valley hushed, fire touching every height,
> While silver brooks in golden rivers meet.
> Then mountains could not check my god-like flight,
> With wild ravine or savage rocky ways;
> But lo, the sea, with warm and tranquil bays,
> Would hold its beauty to my wondering sight.
> And now at length the sun-god seems to sink,
> Yet stirs my heart with new-awakened might,
> The streams of quenchless light I long to drink,
> Before me day and, far behind, the night,
> The heavens above me, and the waves below:
> A lovely dream, but gone with set of sun.
> Ah me, the pinions by the spirit won
> Bring us no flight that mortal clay can know.
> And yet an inborn impulse bids us rise,
> As with an aspiration, constant, strong,
> When, lost from sight in blue and dazzling skies,
> The skylark scatters thrilling shafts of song,

Or when, above the pines and mountain trees,
The eagles wide of pinion veer and sway,
And far across the open plains and seas
The stately cranes will wing their homeward way.'

9 Ernest Jones, *Sigmund Freud: Life and Work* (Hogarth Press 1957), Vol. III, Chapter XIV, 'Occultism', p. 411.

Bollingen, 14th September 1959

Talk after breakfast with C.G. He spoke of Aquarius and the significance of Kruschev's visit to America. He thinks that Kruschev is
getting uneasy because of China; Russia with two hundred million
people is hemmed in between the west and, in the east, China with
six hundred million people; and China won't always do what he
wants. He sees China as a danger.

He was very interested about the Russians hitting the moon and
read every detail in the English papers we had brought with us. He
mentioned later a reference in a Swiss paper to the fact that there was
no proof that they had hit the moon – it could have been a device that
the messages ceased at that time. He had not thought it possible that
the course of the missile could be followed.

15th September 1959

C.G. spoke of Ernest Jones and some of the inaccuracies in his biography of Freud. He said Jones had always been simply a follower
of Freud; he had not added any original ideas. When Jones was writing his book on Freud he never asked him (C.G.) anything about the
early years when he and Freud were working together. As Freud and
Ferenczi were dead C.G. was the only person who could have given
him accurate information, and he could easily have done so. Jones
was not there, and there were a number of errors in his book.

At supper, speaking of his grand-daughter's wedding which was
followed by a feast and a wedding cake, he said, 'You see, there are
always traces of the old things!' The wedding cake is a mandala and
the bride and bridegroom are the royal wedding couple, the King and
Queen, for that evening, and they preside over the gathering. That is
symbolism; it belongs to life.

C.G. said he liked to finish his coffee at breakfast slowly –'I then come to life with no hurry. *"Omnis festinatio a parte diaboli est"*,' he quoted in Latin –'all haste comes from the devil'. It is an old alchemical saying.

I asked him again about the carving of the face of Mercury on the stone at the side of the Tower. He said, 'I got terribly stuck when I was working on synchronicity, in the part about statistics. Then I saw that face in the stone and put my papers away and got my tools and carved it. It was the impish Mercury.' He went on, 'The alchemists knew this hindering thing and Mercury was often mentioned by them as the jester.'

I asked C.G. how Freud had come to think of him as anti-semitic. He told me that he had always talked freely to Freud as to a friend; Freud despised his Jewish associates in Vienna, and he himself had found those in Freud's circle unattractive when he first went to Vienna. There were very few Jews in Switzerland then and no anti-semitism; he had never been anti-semitic.

What he felt about Freud was that he had taken just one of the instincts or drives and tried to explain everything in those terms. He suggested later that the concept of sex was too narrow; there were many other urges, for example nutrition was very important.

His own notion of libido was of mental energy. He wanted Freud to widen his concept to explain facts better. The *concept* (not the theory) was a wide notion: energy was obvious in many ways other than sex, so the concept of energy was, as in physics, a wider one than Freud had conceived. Typology is a description of specific manifestations of energy.

Bergson used the term *élan vital*, but again he was too specific; what is *élan*? It is simply energy and so, said C.G., why not call it that? Bergson used the term as a specific instance of mental energy; but the term energy is not absolutely precise, we don't know what energy is, it is an abstract concept. His own concept of mental energy is not a theory.

Energy is irreversible and goes in one direction, and the goal of energy is no energy – that is *entropy*. The aim of an oak tree is to be an oak tree; it can only grow from below to above, in one direction.

19th September 1959
We left Bollingen and went on to stay at the *Hotel Bad* at Schmerikon.

23rd September 1959
C.G. and Ruth came for dinner at the *Hotel Bad*. He said that he remembered Seif, and that he had been at Munich when Freud fainted. (Seif himself had told me that). I asked if it were true, as Ernest Jones had said, that Seif 'joined' Jung.[1] C.G. said that never happened at all, Seif had joined forces with Adler. (I had met Seif at an Adlerian meeting in London).

26th September 1959
Talk in the afternoon after tea at Bollingen, sitting in the courtyard.

I asked about the effect of Christianity upon non-Christians in Europe, for example the Jews; he had mentioned in *Aion* how the Christian tradition affected people inevitably.[2] He said that amongst the Jews there was, as it were, a parallel effect, for in the *Cabbala* there were similar matters mentioned and the Jews, in a way, were in the Christian tradition.

But of course Christianity was not widespread; there were pockets of Christians. St. Paul's teacher, Gamaliel, was a noted Cabbalist. He said also that for the first thousand years of Christianity (or more) it was quite harmonious and where the 'pockets' or groups were Christianity was fully accepted. Then about 1100 or so came many schisms. This was the spread of knowledge laterally as well as vertically (that is spiritually), and he said he had mentioned this in *Aion*, and that Pisces – he pronounced it with a hard 'c', Piskes – was like this: the sign was a perpendicular and a horizontal fish, they went in opposite directions.[3] And now we are coming to the end of the Pisces era, as was foretold nearly two thousand years ago by the Arabian astrologer Albumasar.[4] The pre-Christian time was Aries.

I asked about the picture which is the frontispiece in *Aion*[5] and he said this meant *the Aion*, the era. This was the Mithraic god, and we know of similar pictures; the god was represented in the temples of

Mithras. The snake is endless time. In a postcard from Arles another picture of Aion was shown together with the signs of the Zodiac; the head of Aion was missing. He said we had practically no written historical records of Mithraism.

I asked about the future of psychology. This he could not foresee – it was conceivable that advances would be made in the field of biochemistry and physiology. It was also possible that our hard-won knowledge of psychology and the psyche and kindred things would be buried for five hundred years.

C.G. had been reading a review in a theological journal from, I think, Czechoslovakia, which criticised him. But, he went on, the theologians seem incapable of seeing what he means, and yet it is quite simple. They resent his intrusion into theology as if it were their private preserve, an area where they alone had special knowledge. Yet we have no such absolute knowledge. They want something to be 'true', just as people deride mythology saying it is not 'true'. He is not interested in the establishment of absolute truth but in observing facts. So far as mythology goes the interesting thing is that *the myths are repeated*, that is a fact and a very important one. But discussing whether the myth is 'true' or not is a waste of time. He would not regard the myth as the dream of a people. Often a myth contained some factual knowledge which 'hit' something, and so it went on, was expressed afresh; such things are important because they are factual. We can have ideas about God; but whether they are 'true' or not, or whether they are 'absolute', cannot be answered. He said he is constantly criticised for saying things which are 'anti-christian' or 'anti-theological', such as all the nonsense about the *privatio boni*.[6]

I asked about *split libido* and he referred to the inevitable polarity of the energic force, its dual nature. So far as introversion or extraversion went they were simple variations, different expressions of energy. But the energy moves in one direction; that is its nature – it does something, or you see something is done.

I asked him about the symbol of the house and in particular the mediaeval house of his dream.[7] 'Well,' he said, 'in a dream we see the house as our husk, and we are just in it.' Thus with the mediaeval house dream he was just there, in this beautiful eighteenth-century house, as he stood on the first floor. It was as if it was where he lived, and presumably his family were about somewhere but they were not evident. When he reflected about it later the house had some association in his mind with his uncle's very old house in Basle which was built in the old moat of the town and had two cellars; the lower one was very dark and like a cave.[8]

In the dream he wondered what was below and went down the steps; near the bottom it was of Roman construction, very old, and in this room were stone slabs for a floor just as there are at Bollingen. There was a ring in one of the stones and this he lifted and went down more steps. The light came in when he lifted this slab. Below he saw bones and skulls and old pottery, all very ancient.

The important thing for him was the stratification, the layers of different ages. This was how he eventually came to the notion of the collective unconscious.

Houses, he said, often came in his dreams. Thus before he took up the study of alchemy he had a dream of a house with two wings quite new to him – he did not know they were there.[9] He looked on this dream as indicating something in his own psychology he did not know about, and the repetition of the dream meant it was being forced to his attention. In his father's room in this house were many zoological specimens in glass vessels; C.G. had earlier a special interest in zoology. In his mother's room were cages, like bird cages, only they were houses, and they were for the ghosts (that is the flitting ideas in the mind) to lodge in. And there were wonderful old books in the library, most lovely manuscripts and old volumes. He associated these also with his uncle's old house in Basle from which he got many books – one a lovely lexicon which he has at Bollingen. This dream was a forerunner of his interest in alchemy. He has often dreamt of houses with additional rooms and this has meant there were many things he had still to find out and that they were there, in 'his house'.

REFERENCES

1 Ernest Jones, *Sigmund Freud: Life and Work* (Hogarth Press 1957), Vol. II, Chapter III, 'The International Psycho-Analytical Association', p. 97.
2 C. G. Jung, *Aion: Researches into the Phenomenology of the Self*, CW Vol. 9, Part II, para. 283: 'I have tried ... to indicate the kind of psychic matrix into which

the Christ-figure was assimilated in the course of the centuries. Had there not been an affinity ... between the figure of the Redeemer and certain contents of the unconscious, the human mind would never have been able to perceive the light shining in Christ and seize upon it so passionately. The connecting link here is the archetype of the God-man, which on the one hand became historical reality in Christ, and on the other, being eternally present, reigns over the soul in the form of a supraordinate totality, the self. The God-man, like the priest in the vision of Zosimos, is ... not only "Lord of the spirits", but "Lord over the (evil) spirits", which is one of the essential meanings of the Christian Kyrios.'

3 *Ibid.*, para. 147: '... The polarity which the fishes acquired may perhaps be due to the fact that the astronomical constellation shows the first (northerly) fish as vertical, and the second (southerly) fish as horizontal. They move almost at right angles to one another and hence form a cross. This counter-movement, which was unknown to the majority of the oldest sources, was much emphasized in Christian times. ...'

4 Albumasar [Abu Ma'shar] (805–85). Arabian astrologer and astronomer whose principal works were printed in Augsburg and Venice at the end of the fifteenth and early sixteenth centuries. In *Aion* Jung quotes from his writings in the chapters on 'The Sign of the Fishes' and 'The Prophecies of Nostradamus'.

5 This is a photograph of a Roman statue of the Mithraic god Aion, of the second or third century, which is in the Vatican Museum in Rome. The god represented the *creative, qualitative principle of time.*

6 The Roman Catholic doctrine of the *privatio boni* was first propounded by Origen (185–254) whose definition of God as the *Summum Bonum* was the effective source for his characterisation of evil as the dimunition of good. The doctrine became established during the early centuries of the Church and was fully developed by Augustine. Jung's empirical observations led him to regard good and evil as opposites of equal reality, and he opposed the doctrine of the *privatio boni*. He writes of it fully in *Aion*, CW Vol. 9, Part II, Chapter V, 'Christ: A Symbol of the Self', paras. 74–80, 89ff, and in the 'Conclusion', paras. 426–28. His point of view is summarised in *Memories, Dreams, Reflections*, Chapter XII, 'Late Thoughts', pp. 303–7; and there are many allusions to the subject in his correspondence with Father Victor White, especially his letter of 31 December 1949, *C. G. Jung: Letters*, Vol. I.

7 See conversation and references 16th January 1952.

8 See conversation and references 16th January 1961.

9 C. G. Jung, *Memories, Dreams, Reflections*, Chapter VII, 'The Work', p. 194.

Küsnacht, 12th January 1961

Arrived in Küsnacht and talked with C.G. before dinner. We spoke of his childhood and he mentioned his early experience of seeing a figure in long dark robes approaching, and his fear at realising that this was not a woman but a man, a Jesuit priest.[1] He said his father was very preoccupied with the Jesuit problem and talked a lot to his friends about it. He (C.G.) was not supposed to be interested in such things but he listened very carefully. When he saw this figure approaching and realised it was a man he was disturbed because he thought it was a man disguised as a woman. There had been a local war in Switzerland in the eighteen-forties. The Roman Catholic Cantons were in conflict against others; they had a battle and even used cannon. The Jesuits were thought to be behind the trouble and to have political aims. Afterwards they were forbidden to wear their habit in Switzerland, or to live in groups such as a community or a monastery. These laws have changed since. Today C.G. had a visit from a Jesuit priest, Pater Rudin; he is the head of a Jesuit Institute in Zürich, and C.G. said this was an Apologetic Institute for Roman Catholic work, and very near the margin of a community.

At dinner Ruth remarked that 'Apologetic' Institute was a curious word to use, as if the Roman Catholic group were being apologetic. C.G. said that in German the word meant *a polite explanation* – it was never used to convey the meaning of being apologetic, this was an English use of the word and a kind of popular misuse of it.

He said Pater Rudin was a serious person who could probably take an independent line about certain problems, such as the *privatio boni*, which was a silly idea in that it conveyed that by thinking the quality of an act could be changed; for example the evil of a murder – but there was the body and no amount of talk would alter it. The Church just could not make things other than they were by saying they were different. Some things were, and remained, evil – like murder; and the British law making self-murder – suicide – a crime was sensible for often the suicide was an alternative to a murder.

He went on to talk about the *Jung Codex*[2] and said there had been some discussion about it. He valued the Gnostics but had thought it better not to keep the *Codex* –'What can I do with it? It's very valuable and has to be kept in a vault in the bank.' So he had given it to the government of Egypt and they were immensely grateful. The Gnostics, who existed before Christianity, interest C.G. very much because they provide an early indication of a recognition of the collective unconscious.

13th January 1961
This morning we (C.G., Ruth Bailey and I, driven by Müller) went above Küsnacht and Meilen to the snow; the fields were all covered but it had melted off the trees. We got out of the car and walked; it was pretty cold.

Later, in the afternoon, I had tea with Mrs. Niehus. She made an interesting point that her father's books became more difficult as he had grown older because he always wrote from the point of view of his age – that is his thought had proceeded and younger people sometimes found it difficult to understand what he was getting at. This comment struck me as relevant to some of the criticisms that C.G.'s writings are obscure; it is not necessarily that he is obscure but that his thought constantly develops, and he sees the subject differently and writes from that point of view, the angle of an older person. While we were out this morning he remarked on the difference it made to younger people when their parents died for then there was no one ahead of them, they themselves were in the front rank in Time.

In the evenings, last night and tonight, we have sat in the library. I asked C.G. about the inscription carved over the door of the house: *Vocatus atque non vocatus Deus aderit*, a saying taken from the Latin translation by Erasmus of the words of the Delphic oracle. C.G. found the little book and showed it to me. It is bound in vellum and is small, about six inches by three, and thick. On the spine it reads: *Erasmi R Adagiorum EPITOME 1563*. Inside is the full printed title. His dates are 1466–1536, so the date of the book, *Epitome*, was after his death. On p. 432 of this little volume is the following: '*Vocatus atque non vocatus Deus aderit : Oraculum olim Lacedaemoniis, redittum, abiit, in proverbium.*' There followed some lines of Greek in the Byzantine cursive writing which C.G. transcribed for me.

For the rest of the evening we sat, C.G. with his feet up reading or playing patience, and Ruth reading my manuscript on the couch; my chair is by the table (as on previous visits) and I write or read – with a rather bad light too.

14th January 1961

At breakfast C.G. spoke of Freud and recalled remarking to him, 'Psycho-analysis and its principles are very good for patients but not so good for the analyst.' He was amazed at Freud's reply, 'Of course not, that's quite true.' He said that Freud could come out of the medical (professional) part of his house and close that door; then he was in his family and that had nothing to do with analysis. He said the Freudian system was dominated by the mother complex; it was not a psychology which took in women – Freud got stuck in the Oedipus complex. C.G. had suggested to him the need for some psychological understanding of women and mentioned the Jocasta idea.[3]

Later I asked again about the book by Erasmus and the mention in the quotation of the Lacedaemonians. 'Oh yes,' he said, 'the Lacedaemonians were going to attack Athens and they consulted the Delphic oracle to see how the battle would go.' He said the writing on the spine of the book was a mistake. He translated the Latin (quoted above): 'An oracle given to the Lacedaemonians became a proverb: "Called or not called the God will be present".' One can apply it where we want to hint at something that may be, but has not been, solicited, something that may happen in future whether we want it or not, such as old age or death – an inevitable fate. He mentioned that the story of the Lacedaemonians consulting the oracle before battle was paralleled in the Old Testament; God was consulted before battle also and God would warn them of his wrath. I think it was Hosea he referred to when God pushed the righteous under his chair and slew the others.

We talked of the *Ehrenbürger* ceremony[4] and he was very pleased with it; he has the right of voting in the Council. The document they presented to him hangs in the hall. C.G. said the term *Ehrenbürgerrecht* was correct; but this document has 'C. G. JUNG' raised in gold lettering and also '*Bürgerrecht*' in gold.

I am sitting now in the study on the couch with C.G. in his chair on my right reading my manuscript, commenting and making a few alterations in pencil.

15th January 1961

C.G., Ruth and I went for a drive leaving the Seestrasse at 10 a.m. We went into Zürich and on to the lovely old town of Baden – much industrialised, and to Meiringen; then to Bremgarten, and finally on the Albis Pass where numbers of people were engaged in winter sports – a very large area with good slopes and quite long runs, a ski-lift, and youngsters tobogganing. *Very* cold air. It is only about 2,500 feet up, but that's quite a lot. From there we went back to Zürich and on to Küsnacht arriving in time for lunch.

I went for a walk after lunch to the pier at the Strandbad while the others slept.

After tea again I sat on the couch in the study more or less behind C.G. while he read my manuscript and made comments, of which I took some notes. It was difficult to do this as he talked but I wrote down all I could.

After supper Ruth went on with her reading of it, which she is doing now. I am sitting by the table in the study and have been reading Herbert Read's book, *The Forms of Things Unknown*. C.G. read this book right through hoping at each chapter to find out what Read thought; it never comes through and he goes on quoting other people instead.

16th January 1961

C.G. said the Tower was one of the first places he visited in London. I asked about the ravens but he didn't recall them.

Laurens van der Post came for lunch. He spoke of his recent visit to South Africa and other parts of Africa. He referred to the Dutch Church as non-Christian and recalled as a boy seeing his mother in a Dutch Reformed Church receiving the Holy Communion from a black clergyman, and in that Church they hand the cup from one to another. She received it from a coloured person on her left and, having partaken herself, handed it on to another coloured person on her right. But now all that has gone. He spoke of the Zulu farewell – 'Go on your way without haste'.[5]

In the evening, between half past five and six, in the study alone with C.G., and he is reading my manuscript. ... His mother's house in Basle: she was not born there but lived in it throughout her childhood. It was the house of the priest at Basle Cathedral, and last year they did some excavations and alterations in it and found that it had been built on Roman remains, and underneath there was a cellar just like that in his dream of the mediaeval house.[6] This interested him very much – that somehow it was in the family. This old house appears in the picture of the 'Basle Broadsheet' in his book on *Flying Saucers*.[7]

Ruth had shown me a photograph of C.G. today, taken on the balcony outside the 'blue room', and she has just asked him if I can use it as the frontispiece to my book – I had told her I would like to do so – and he has agreed. She will have a copy made and get C.G. to sign it and then send it to me.

Later in the evening Ruth read from the paper an account of a man in Bristol who collided with a wall on his motor cycle, was thrown over it, landed on the back of a horse which bolted, and half way across the field he fell off – unhurt. C.G. was very interested.

17th January 1961

C.G. has finished reading my book; he told me it read easily and that he thought highly of it, so that is satisfactory.

At lunch C.G. mentioned that he had just heard an extraordinary story from a friend, a doctor, who came to see him this morning. He had told him of a car he had which was 'pixillated' (that is 'had a gremlin'). The car belonged to him, and when his wife drove it she had accidents of such an unusual kind that he decided to sell the car to a garage. It had been smashed up in the last accident but the garage owner repaired it; then when driving it he was killed! Previously the couple had had a series of accidents. For example as they were driving along an open road the car suddenly skidded on a perfectly safe surface – there was no question of rain or ice; it skidded to the left and then into a lamp post on the right and was smashed up. The driver of a following car stopped and asked what on earth had happened as there was no apparent reason for the accident, and neither the doctor nor his wife could explain it. The same thing had happened before on an alpine road when again his wife was driving. There was plenty of room and they were following some army trucks; then the truck in front of them pulled up. The doctor shouted to his wife to swing left instantly – she just missed the lorry but it was a very close shave and they could easily have crashed over the edge of the road. The trouble, C.G. said, lay in the wife, and then her animus has a negative effect upon her husband; his only safe line (said C.G.) was not to react at all. I remarked that the story was rather like the crash in the bookcase during the conversation between Freud and himself. 'Yes,' he said, 'that's it exactly.'

I left the Seestrasse at 1.20 and got a bus from the Air Terminal which reached Kloten at 2.5. The buses go frequently and one can take any of them and then simply wait at Kloten until the plane departs, as I am now doing.

[Here, at Zürich airport, the notes come to an end, for these six days in January 1961 were the last my husband spent with Professor Jung, whose death occurred a few months later, on the 6th June. F.E.B.]

REFERENCES

1   See conversation of 21 March 1959, reference 3.
2   Summer 1955, reference 3.
3   In Greek legend Jocasta was the wife of Laïus, and mother (later also wife) of Oedipus.
4   The ceremony at which Jung received the Freedom of the Village of Küsnacht.
5   In commenting on this conversation Sir Laurens van der Post added: 'What I told them was that the Zulus in taking leave of one another use an expression which literally translated means, "May you go slowly", but idiomatically, "Go in happiness". It means that idiomatically because the Zulus believe that all evil comes from haste and that if man goes through life slowly, all that is good will be drawn to him.'
6   See conversation of 16th January 1952, reference 7.
7   C. G. Jung, *Flying Saucers: A Modern Myth of Things Seen in the Skies*, p. 128, Figure I: 'Basle Broadsheet, 1566'. The house mentioned is that on the right.
    See also C. G. Jung, *Civilization in Transition*, CW Vol. 10, V, *Flying Saucers*; the 'Basle Broadsheet' is reproduced as Plate V.

Also from DAIMON ZÜRICH

A Testament to the Wilderness consists of ten international responses to a highly original paper by Swiss psychiatrist C. A. Meier. This colorful collection of authors views wilderness within and without, psychologically and ecologically, presenting a wealth of perspectives on an ancient – and at the same time eminently relevant – phenomenon.

Published with The Lapis Press.

ISBN 3-85630-503-3

The Myth of Meaning is a classic work by the well-known co-author of C. G. Jung's «Memories, Dreams, Reflections». Still working and writing in the tradition of Jung today, Aniela Jaffé here elaborates on the vital role played by meaning – or its absence – in every human life. This book can help us to more awareness of our own – collective as well as personal – myths of meaning.

ISBN 3-85630-500-4